# GET CONNECTED

The Social Networking Toolkit
# FOR BUSINESS

# GET CONNECTED

## The Social Networking Toolkit
# FOR BUSINESS

**Starr Hall**
Chadd Rosenberg

**EP**
**Entrepreneur. Press**

Publisher: Jere L. Calmes
Cover Design: Del LeMond
Production and Editorial Services: CWL Publishing Enterprises, Inc.,
Madison, WI, www.cwlpub.com

This publication is designed to provide accurate and authoritative information in regard to the subject matter covered. It is sold with the understanding that the publisher is not engaged in rendering legal, accounting,
or other professional services. If legal advice or other expert assistance is
required, the services of a competent professional person should be
sought.

ISBN 13: 978-1-59918-358-9
     10: 1-59918-358-7

**Library of Congress Cataloging-in-Publication Data**

Rosenberg, Chadd.
   Get connected : the social networking toolkit for business / by Chadd
Rosenberg and Starr Hall.
     p. cm.
   ISBN 1-59918-358-7 (alk. paper)
   1. Business networks. 2. Social networks. I. Hall, Starr. II. Title.
   HD69.S8.R674 2009
   006.7'54068—dc22

                                                        2009011764

Printed in Canada
13 12 11 10 09                              10 9 8 7 6 5 4 3 2 1

# Contents

# Contents

# Contents

# Contents

# Foreword

 **If** you're wondering what it takes to grow a business in today's environment, online marketing and social networking are proving to be the fastest, most efficient ways to reach and connect with current and new customers, sometimes into the millions.

My personal passion in reaching customers and clients around the globe via teleseminars and online virtual book tours brought me into this new world of branding—social networking. It is apparent that the social media environment is a great place to market and grow your business. What started as a fad has now transitioned into a movement that continues to have a huge yet positive impact on a company's bottom line, its brand recognition, and customer loyalty.

The difference between a company that succeeds online and one that doesn't is whether managers and business owners understand how to use these new media tools efficiently. Although the World Wide Web is evolving daily and new social networking sites may come and go, the importance of joining the conversation and incorporating this strategy into your marketing plan now is crucial to the long-term success of any business.

This book is a great step-by-step and reference guide to get you up and running with social networking, and it will save you hundreds of hours in research and training. The chapters start right off with how-tos and fresh and innovative approaches and ideas to using social networking as a marketing tool. With reviews of the top social networking sites that include step-by-step set up information, site tips, tricks, and resources, this book is not only for beginners. It's also a good book for bringing experienced social networkers up to speed on some new techniques, sites, and resources. Use this book as a guide or tutorial. Whichever way you decide to use it, it will serve you well in future learning and in your day-to-day social networking.

Starr Hall and Chadd Rosenberg have written an educational and easy-to-understand book with the purpose of teaching entrepreneurs and business owners how to navigate through all of the hype and focus in on tested and proven online networking techniques. The book includes everything you need to know to get started with social networking as well as how to grow your business online.

You will be able to clearly identify your online networking goals, create a plan, be efficient with your time, and choose what sites are best for you and your company. Furthermore, the book includes actual case history success stories that will help you learn a few additional secrets to social networking greatness.

It's my pleasure to provide this foreword and to recommend this book. I resonate with this book's simplicity and Starr Hall's obvious passion for social networking. It is apparent that Starr is a social networking and media expert and a darn good educator.

I enjoyed the book and found it valuable. I think you will, too. Enjoy!

P.S. If you have a sales and or marketing staff, I encourage you to get a book for every team member. You'll be glad you did.

—Alex Mandossian
Founder, www.HeritageHouseMedia.com

# Preface

 started as a conversation online several years ago. I was browsing through my e-mail in-box, and I came across an invite from a long-time contact and friend to join them on LinkedIn. My first thought was, what in the heck is LinkedIn, and why do I need to go to that site to talk to this person? Why can't they just e-mail me? So, I ignored the e-mail. A few weeks passed, and I received another LinkedIn invite. Only this time it was from the head of a major corporation. I sat back and wondered, why is the CEO of this company on a site trying to talk and connect with me? There must be something more to this that I'm missing. That is when my fascination with social networking began.

Hello, my name is Starr Hall, and I am a social networking addict! What started out as an e-mail invite turned into a two-way online conversation that transitioned into new business for me that continues to this day. I became so involved with online social networks that I actually stopped doing tradition-al marketing and networking for almost a year. I just had to go to every site I could find to see if I wanted to be on it—and, more importantly, if my ideal client and/or target market was on the site. Through the contacts I made, I began to receive requests for paid speaking engagements and consulting client contracts, and my e-mail list tripled in a matter of months. I was so excited about all of my continued successes that I started to share them both online and off. It was then that I realized I was the only one in my circle and center of influence who was reaping the benefits of this new phenomenon.

I started to watch other postings and asked managers and entrepreneurs who were online what type of business they were getting and what were some of their secrets for getting this business through social networking sites. Only a few major networkers online had successful stories and case histories that they could share. I wondered what in the heck everyone else was even doing online if they weren't getting the business from it. Where they just there to gossip and chat? I certainly didn't have time for that.

Within the first few months of my social networking experiences, I just knew that I had to write a book to help businesses and entrepreneurs not only learn about social networks but learn how to actually get business from their online conversations and efforts and not get caught up in gossip and often useless chatter.

I really started to see a shift with social networking with the Obama campaign. I truly believe that Obama and his campaign team changed the face of social networking by taking it from a conversation to an engaging and interactive branding and business-building tool. I followed the online campaign from start to finish and incorporated some of Obama's techniques and approaches into my own networking online. It worked!

This book is not just a how-to resource guide. Every page incorporates countless hours of research and experience to show you how and why social networking works and why you should incorporate this medium into your current and future marketing strategy. I'm passionate about social networking and what it can do for businesses, and I've shared all my secrets and findings with you throughout this book. If you use this book as a reference and resource guide to help you along your social networking journey, I assure you that you will achieve online branding success. Remember that the key to action is being persistent. Don't jump on a site and try it for a week and then decide that it doesn't work. Just as it takes time to build in-person relationships and business, the same applies online. The difference is you can access more people, faster and home in on your actual ideal client and or target market.

I just could not keep these techniques and tips to myself another minute. I had to get them into print for you, and I am so glad that Entrepreneur Press shared the same passion by choosing to publish this book and get it out there for you and everyone interested in social networking and its marketing potential.

I have been in branding since early childhood. I was, raised in a family that started and branded the craft industry from the mid 1940s. Marketing and branding is what I do and what I know, and every time I find a new way to grow a business, whether it's through technology or media, I become obsessed with finding out everything I need to know to help my clients. I think of you as a client. You bought my book, and I am truly grateful for that.

I suggest you use this book not only as a reference guide but a tool to learn how to extend your social networking presence and the marketing potential that comes from it. Become active on the sites where you can reach your target market, and leave the rest behind. Treat your online connections just as you would in-person ones. The only difference is the basic understanding of each online community in which you operate and the fact that you can speak to hundreds, thousands, even millions of people at a time through social networking.

Technology is flying toward us at what sometimes seems like the speed of light. Social networking sites may come and go, but the online arena and conversations are here to stay. They will continue to evolve into better, bigger, and more user-friendly tools for you to grow your business. Therefore, it's important that you stay active online and have a consistent presence.

Try not to get overwhelmed with all of the information in this book (because there is a lot). Just take in what makes sense for you and go at your own pace. The great thing is that you have this book and have made the commitment to learn the basics or expand your knowledge in this important new area for connecting to customers. If you have employees, buy them a copy or pass this one onto them. You will want to make sure that you start to train your entire team in social networking because it will be vital in the years to come in growing your business. Studies have shown in two years that approximately 50% of all new business will come from online connections. Be ready now and get connected.

So let's get started!

—Starr Hall
International Speaker, Author,
and Publicist, www.starrhall.com

# Acknowledgments

## From Starr Hall

My name is on the front cover, but many others were absolutely essential in the creation of *Get Connected, The Social Networking Toolkit for Businesses*. Chadd Rosenberg, a long time friend, did the initial research along with his wife, Brittany. How they put up with me during this process I'll never know. I found much of my inspiration as well as content for this book from my clients and their active campaigns, and I thank them for this. I spent many nights online doing research, testing, interviewing, navigating and yes, some times forgetting that it was ten o'clock, and I had to feed my family. My amazing children, Austin, 19, Savannah, 16, and Jackson, 10, were so patient with me during my endless social networking and research, and they brought me great laughter during the process.

In this book, I can share real-world experiences and valuable content and find the right words to communicate on how to build a brand, using this tool. But I find that I have no words to express how grateful I am for Heidi Borchers, my mother and best friend. Her gifts make the world a more creative and better place, and have enriched the lives of those lucky enough to know her. Without her support, this book and my international tour would not be possible. A special thank you to all of you for picking up this book and committing to get connected through social networking.

Stay social a great line from my friend Chris Patterson, www.InSocialMedia.com.

## From Chadd Rosenberg

To Eric Elkins of Wide Focus (www.widefoc.us), thank you for your valuable expertise and time. As a social media expert and pioneer, who spends every minute of the day helping corporations build and understand their online presence, we appreciate all the advice and content you donated to this project. You

## Acknowledgments

helped turn a good idea into a real book. Brittany Rosenberg, thank you for the hours of editing, putting up with the late nights and weekends spent working on this book, and for putting up with our last minute requests.

# About the Authors

**Starr Hall** is an international publicist and social networking efficiency expert. She has worked with national and international corporations, non-profit organizations, authors, CEOs, and associations. She has relationships with over 800 editors, writers, and segment producers worldwide and has secured placement and coverage for her clients in regional, national, and international newspapers, magazines, radio, television, and internet outlets. In addition, she has secured major book, co-branding and licensing contracts for her clients worldwide. With hundreds of client recommendations and media endorsements, Starr is known for getting her clients massive media coverage and creating word of mouth buzz through social networking media for brands worldwide. She is a regularly featured columnist for Entrepreneur.com and *Central Coast Magazine* as well as the host of a successful talk radio show, *Keeping Company with Starr Hall*. Visit her website at **starrhall.com**.

**Chadd Hall.** A born "people-person," and a graduate of Arizona State University, Chadd Hall has been coaching and helping people succeed his entire life. A veteran entrepreneur with multiple small businesses, his experience with 21st century promotion has come through the music industry and corporate podcasting. After returning to school for an audio engineering degree from California Recording Institute, he opened and ran a recording studio (Studio 154) for seven years. He founded his current company, New World of Media, in 2006, which produces audio and video content for corporate clients and distributes it through a variety of new and traditional media outlets. His studio has created commercial music for clients such as MTV, Fox, ESPN, TLC, Subaru, and Mitsubishi. His podcasting clients range from high-tech start ups to major public relations firms including IBM, Qualys, ESET, Yola, Schwartz Communications and Citigate-Cunningham. Visit his website at **newworldofmedia.com**.

# Introduction to Social Networking

 is social networking? At the most basic level the definition of social networking is to take traditional or in-person networking activities online. The internet and networking have come along way. When the internet first took notice in the mid to late 1990s the online experience was mainly an individual endeavor. Today, the internet includes networking with chat, video, and pictures. You can reconnect with lost friends, college roommates, past lovers, or even communicate with the rich and famous. Perhaps most importantly, however, social networking has become a way to increase your connections and generate business.

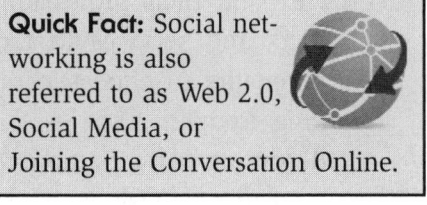

**Quick Fact:** Social networking is also referred to as Web 2.0, Social Media, or Joining the Conversation Online.

## The Internet Is Part of Our Lives

Today the internet is a part of just about everyone's life. We use this tool to do everything from keeping in touch and booking

**Note:** We'll be discussing various types of new technology. If you're just starting out with social networking, keep the glossary handy.

1

plane tickets to conducting research. Social networking offers internet users a new dimension by allowing people with similar interests and activities to form online communities. The rise of video streaming, blogs, wikis, and bookmarking sites has enhanced the concept of social networks.

You begin by posting a personal profile or resume online, which serves as an introduction to other members. From there, you can exchange information, opinions, photos, or videos with other users. You can also self-publish your thoughts in a blog, chat in real time with others, and tag other sites of interest. It's also possible to define your degree of interaction with others by selecting whether to network in a public setting where anyone can join or to participate in a private, invitation-only group.

Today, small business owners are embracing social networking as a means of building professional connections, generating awareness, developing new sales prospects, and recruiting employees. There are many benefits to joining the conversation online within social networks. These sites are powered by active communities of like-minded people. By tapping into these communities, small-business owners can not only expand their professional networks, but promote their products and services to targeted segments. We encourage entrepreneurs to choose carefully when engaging social-networking groups.

Becoming part of a community whose members resemble your customer base is a smart way to get your business noticed. Consider adding a blog, photos related to your business, and a viral video campaign to your social-networking profile—blogs display your professional savvy, while online videos and photos offer a low-cost way to drive business to your doorstep.

Since social networking lets you build sales beyond your local geographic area, it's more than just an excellent complement to your more regional marketing efforts. Combine the rapid pace of the online world with the tight-knit character of online social networks, and you have the potential to expand your business through what some call word of mouse.

> **Quick Fact:** Ning is an online platform for users to create their own social websites and social networks whether it's for your industry, cause, or organization. *Ning* is a Chinese surname that means peace.

# Types of Social Networking Sites

Though this is by no means an exhaustive list, here's a general breakdown of the types of social media sites you may consider using. Don't get overwhelmed by the number of sites out there, just remember this general rule: You only need to start with two or three of these to effectively market your business. These include:

- Social networks:
  Facebook
  MySpace
  Hi5
  Bebo
  Friendster
  Xanga
  Twitter
  Tagged
  Blitztime
  A vast array of Ning platform networks

- Professional networks:
  LinkedIn
  Plaxo
  Xing
  Zoominfo
  Spoke
  Social News

- Social bookmarking:
  Digg
  Delicious
  StumbleUpon

- Forums
  Meetup
  Craigslist

- Business directories:
  Yelp
  CitySearch

- Photo, video sharing, and live chat:
  YouTube
  Flickr

# Networking Review

It's the second half of the phrase in social networking so it is obvious that this would be one of its uses. Networking online is resembles networking offline, only without geographical boundaries and finding new people to network with requires only a keyword search. If you have ever gone to a business "mixer" or trade show conference, you have likely networked before. Think about all the time and effort it took just to get a handful of key business contacts. The travel, hotels, rental cars expenses just so you could collect a couple hundred business cards—and that's if you were really working the floor. Furthermore, when you return to the office you have a couple hundred followup e-mails and

**Groups:** Nearly every site has groups organized by common interests. Search for every possible group that you might be interested in and join as many as the site or your time will allow. This is the easiest way to widen your circle of influence, gain exposure, find strategic partners, get customers, and narrow the focus of whom you want to connect with. You'll learn specifics about joining groups and using them to your advantage later in the book.

phone calls to make if you have any chance of building a quality relationship with these new contacts.

Even at the local events you have to dedicate several hours of your time telling stories, shaking hands, and realizing halfway through the hour-long conversation that you have no reason to be talking with this person! Social networking makes this process more effective and efficient by giving you access to tens of millions of people all attending the world's largest mixer 24 hours a day, 7 days a week, 365 days a year. All you need to do to attend is join the site of your choice and log in. We'll share tips with you throughout this book to not only help you get started but help you stay on a business growth path.

Mark Twain once said, "It's better to keep your mouth shut and appear stupid, than to open it up and remove all doubt." The same could be said when entering the world of blogs, micro-blogs, and other postings one may come across on social networks. The general rule is to listen (or read) first. You'll learn more by observing than by jumping into the conversation immediately. You will also likely avoid making you and your business look like the newbie you are.

Have you ever been told (probably on more than one occasion) "It never hurts to ask"? In the case of social networking, this absolutely applies. In fact, asking questions is probably the best way to initiate conversations on social networks. Too many people make the mistake of joining a new site and posting as much information about their business in as many places as they can find.

While this tactic may get you greater exposure, it will not build trust or foster any sense of connection with the rest of the social network. When we started our social networking campaign for Starr Hall Inc. we began with a simple question, "How can we help?" On each site, in each group we posted something similar to, "Hi, I'm Starr Hall. I have built brands worldwide through public relations and social networking branding including A-list media placement. I'm not here to brag, just here to help." If you use these three simple techniques—find your groups of interest, listen first, then ask questions—your initial experiences with social networking will most likely be positive and productive.

# Getting Started

Now that you're armed with a few simple tips to get started, let's look at how you can develop your business. If you're reading this book you're probably not doing so to become more popular, your goal is most likely to build your business. That means getting more customers, right? Well, not exactly. Online social networks don't respond well to one-way messaging. For example, a company places a television ad that will reach 20 million people. This ad message is one-way to their target market; however, it doesn't allow potential consumers to message back or participate in what is called two-way messaging. Two-way messaging is what engages potential customers. It allows them to give their feedback, feel involved, or better yet, a part of the business or brand. This is what builds credibility and trust and why social networking works!

You simply need to accept that traditional methods of gaining exposure and therefore customers through the use of passive ads (Yellow Pages, newspaper, radio, TV) and direct marketing (postcard mailers, cold calls) just don't work in this wired world like they used to pre-internet. Sharing information, giving advice, asking questions, reviews, and referrals: These are the tools of the social networker. You'll get specific examples of how to do this in the case study chapters in this book. Many of the businesses we interviewed no longer use any form of advertising or direct marketing. For them, social networking is their only new-business development activity.

A successful social networking strategy will put your business in front of millions of new people, for a lot less time and money than the company that spends thousands, even millions, of dollars for a TV ad to reach 20 million people. Gaining widespread visibility is still a good thing, but there must be more to it than that. People today want to interact with the brands that they value, they want a sense of community and to feel that you are like them.

Customers not only want to trust the brands they buy but have the ability to influence their future progress. CEOs of major companies are blogging with customers about their experience with a given product and seeking advice on ways to improve it. To build your business through social networks you have to give of yourself, your knowledge, and advice; then receive the knowledge and advice of others. As your network grows, and this reciprocal exchange of ideas progresses, the customers will come.

# How to Use Social Networking for Your Business

 networking is not just for teenagers, there are now serious sites with powerful tools to build your business. This chapter explains various business uses of social networking. Most small business owners don't use terms like *reputation management*, *top-of-mind branding*, and *key influencers*, but now is the time. These aren't only marketing terms, they have real meaning to your business even if you're an entrepreneur working out of your home (like me!). This chapter will show you how to employ the same techniques that large corporations use to stay on top by using social networking.

## Choosing the Best Sites for Your Business

The social network explosion means choosing from a lengthy list of sites. Social networks exist for every interest and agenda, however not all are appropriate for your business or cause. Here are a few tips on getting started:

- Start with two of the most popular sites: Facebook and LinkedIn. Setting up a profile on these two sites will give you a taste of social networks while allowing you to interact with potential customers, cause community members, and business partners. Consider joining specialized or targeted sites that are specific to your industry or area of interest. These are focused on more specific interests, as opposed to general social-networking destinations.

- After joining, continue to stay active and monitor your preferred social networks as well as new ones that come online. It's important that your goals and potential customer base are reflected in the social networks that you choose.

## Reputation Building and Management

Wikipedia defines *reputation management* as "the process of tracking an entity's actions and other entities' opinions about those actions; reporting on those actions and opinions; and reacting to that report creating a feedback loop. All entities involved are generally people, but that need not always be the case. Other examples of entities include animals, businesses, or even locations or materials. The tracking and reporting may range from word-of-mouth to statistical analysis of thousands of data points."

**Quick Fact:** Wikipedia is a free, multilingual encyclopedia site project operated by the nonprofit Wikimedia Foundation. The word *wiki* is from the Hawaiian word *wiki*, meaning quick and *pedia* from the word *encyclopedia*.

For our purposes we're only concerned with the reputations of people and businesses. Of course, to manage your reputation you have to have one. Social networks provide an international stage to show off your shiny new dress. Just watch out for the paparazzi taking pictures of your undergarments, or lack thereof! It's important to remember that customers will form and share their opinions about you and your business with or without you. Wouldn't you rather join that conversation?

I've heard so many businesses say they don't think that they need to be social networking. Restaurants are the biggest offenders. They claim they only need to focus on customers coming from around their town or even a small region. They don't worry about a statewide or even national reputation. Unless they're in a town small enough where everyone knows everyone else and all of those people are spreading positive word of mouth about the restaurant, then they're headed for trouble. How did you used to look for a restaurant in your area? Maybe the Yellow Pages or a recommendation from a friend or co-worker? Well now these people and search systems are online. People look for restaurants, read about experiences, and talk about them. These restaurant need to invest some time to get up and running on these sites and create a system to monitor and stay involved. Or they can spend hundreds—even thousands—per month to advertise in their local Yellow Pages. For what? Other than the location, hours of operation, and a self-proclaimed "We're the best/quickest/cheapest in town" there is little information of value.

## Google and Yahoo!

Google and Yahoo! have changed the way we look for businesses. They not only provide a handy map, but a look at those undergarments, as well. Sites like Citysearch and Yelp allow users to review local businesses and post their feelings to the world. This has a profound effect for our local restaurant in question. It used to be that all a restaurateur would have to worry about was the one night a year when the food critic from the local newspaper stopped by. Treat them to your finest meal on the house, keep the wine

**Map:** In many programming languages, a *map* is the name of a higher-order function that applies a given function to a sequence of elements (such as a list) and returns a sequence of results, kind of like a key word search.

flowing, and pray for a good review. By the way, the number of people who are reading the daily paper nowadays continues to decline. Consumers are now posting their reviews and culinary experiences online. With social networking in the mix, now every single customer, each and every night, is a possible food critic. Their review may have the same reach and impact, but unlike the article, it won't go in the recycle bin the next day. Online reviews are there for good or at least for the life of the participants' posting account being active.

The map function on Google and Yahoo! pulls in reviews from external sites like Yelp and Citysearch, among others, to provide added value for their loyal searchers. If you haven't seen this for yourself, go to Google maps, type the name of your city, then type sushi or pizza or any popular type of food. Where would you rather go: "Jim's Second Day Sushi ... 2 stars" or "Fresh as Can Be Fish ... 4½ stars"? Hmm ... tough choice. Unfortunately for Jim, that ranking is an average of the reviews posted. So while he may actually run a fine, clean, safe establishment, albeit with an odd name, his reputation could be sullied with only a few bad reviews.

Since we're still in the early part of this trend most local businesses have less than 10 reviews. That's hardly a fair and representative sample. There's an old business saying that proclaims on average a happy customer will tell three people, but an unhappy one will tell seven. Well what if that unhappy customer has the ability to reach 7,000 or, worse, 700,000? In any case, it's important that your business be properly registered with these search sites and at a minimum that you occasionally monitor what, if anything, is being said about you and your business.

Whether you're building your reputation in groups on LinkedIn, Twittering your way to notoriety, or procuring positive reviews on Yelp, it's vital that you understand the role Key Influencers play in your success or failure. For example, a 13-year-old boy who lives for punk rock, video games, and skateboarding *and* has 5,000 friends on Myspace could be a key influencer to a variety of youth and extreme sports-oriented companies.

Key influencers can be any of the following: journalists, industry analysts, celebrities, politicians, bloggers, academics, retailers, manufacturers. The fact is they can be almost anyone. Your job is to find who they are in your industry and in your region, as well. Get to know these people, track their actions on social networks, make friends with them if you can. Key influencers hold treasure chests of thousands, even millions of people who value their opinion. If you launch a product, and they review and endorse it, you've avoided the expensive process of reaching out to those people yourself and convincing them of your product's worth.

Given the limited number of reviews most small businesses get, anyone who posts about your business on Yelp or Citysearch is a de-facto key influencer. Engage them, thank those who submit positive reviews and you can even offer them something exclusive like VIP access or maybe a discount. Also, thank those who submit negative reviews. Respond to their concerns, as well. You shouldn't try to convince or change someone's mind, just let them know that you heard and respect their voice and would like to give them a chance to engage with you further.

> **Quick Fact:** *A key influencer* is any person who has influence of a large number of people. They can be potential buyers or current customers.

I went to a nightclub recently that I have had a positive experience with in the past, but it was poorly reviewed online. I asked to speak to the manager, and told him that people on Yelp were complaining about the lack of friendliness from the staff and that there was a high likelihood of a fight breaking out at some point in the night. I explained that I had not had this experience, but wanted to know if he was aware of the perception, whether deserving or not. He did not know and said he would address it. That week I saw a post on their MySpace page announcing that they were aware of the problems and had taken steps to rectify them. More security and smiling bartenders were evident on our next visit about a month later.

Your customers have moved online. Yes, you have a website, but that's not enough anymore. You need to build and mange your reputation online to succeed in today's marketplace. Social networking provides the perfect set of tools to get the job done.

# Become an Expert in Your Field

It wasn't very long ago when the only "well-known experts" were the talking heads commenting on CNN panels or quoted in newspaper articles. Today experts are self-made and can be found online on a variety of blogs and social networks like LinkedIn and Twitter. Some, like LinkedIn and eBay, provide point systems to earn your way to desired levels of expertise. It's like being granted an honorary Ph.D. from a university.

At first you should be asking anyone and everyone questions or posting questions in groups for feedback. They can be about almost anything: I'm confused, can someone tell me what a Wiki is? Can anyone recommend a good search engine optimization company? Or, All the social networking on my computer is causing me to gain weight ... any thoughts on how to get my social networking to go? The more questions you ask the better you'll be able to discern how questions get answered on social networks. When you feel comfortable you should start answering questions or start discussions in groups or forums. If people like your answers, you'll quickly become known as people share your advice with others. Before you know it, you're an expert!

You don't have to wait for a question to share your knowledge. One of the best ways to increase your expert ranking on many sites is to give away free tips. Top five lists are great because they provide just enough information to be valuable, but still fit within the confines of a reasonable post. If they don't, consider linking to an area on your website or blog that has all the pertinent information and leave just the summary on the posting.

Post everywhere. If you have something to say, maximize its effect and your time by posting it to numerous outlets. Copy and paste to your blog, e-mail list, all your social network profiles and to all of the groups you belong to. To further build your e-mail list, offer a free report from the post and have an e-mail capture on your blog where people need to go to enter their name and e-mail to get the free report. One top five list could be placed in over a hundred places reaching hundreds of thousands of people. This may sound like a lot of work but with the proper organization and automation you should be able to complete a task like this in under an hour. Think of the cost of placing an ad that would reach the same number of people.

Are you getting the picture that joining groups is a good idea? You should. It's repeated in almost every section of this book. So why not repeat it again: Groups! Groups! Groups!

You may only have a few hundred friends or connections on your profile but a popular group may have 10,000 members. Anything you post to that group will be seen eventually by every single one of them the next time they log in. This exponential reach will enable you to build your expert status floor by floor rather than brick by brick.

# Money vs. Time

 **You** are either going to spend time or money to build your network and business. You can pay someone to market and build your business or you can put marketing time and effort into building it yourself. In almost all cases signing up on a social network is free. Some will offer premium services for a small fee, but most people and businesses will never need them. What social networking does require is time. In some cases, depending on your focus and campaign goals, it may take a lot of time.

## Traditional Marketing vs. Social Networking

Now before you throw the book down and start yelling to no one in particular that you don't have extra time; let me offer some perspective. Traditional forms of advertising and marketing still take time to create and are incredibly costly. Additionally, the traditional media outlets where these ads would be placed have lost their influence. Here are a few examples.

- **Yellow Pages:** Print ads in this publication can expire the minute they go to print and are very costly. If you're a business, such as locksmith, lawyer, emergency service, or a tow truck driver, keep your full-page ads; the rest of you should save your money.

17

- **Newspapers:** Circulation—down, ad rates—up! The loyal subscribers who are reading the daily newspaper are doing so for the *articles*, not your tiny business card advertisement. Unless you're committed to consistent, long-term advertising to keep your name out there, this medium isn't nearly as effective as it used to be. Ad sales reps always like to talk about reach, or how many people your ad will potentially be seen by. They will say, "Total circulation is 150,000, for only $500 you can have a quarter page ad." Yes, but for how long, one day? A week at best. How many of those 150,000 papers won't be read at all? How many people will actually see your ad in the 50-plus pages? How many will not only see your ad, but actually read it? Finally, how many will take action after reading your ad by taking down the phone number and calling?

- **Cable Television:** Three letters say it all, DVR. Who watches the commercials on any other day than the Super bowl? Okay, I like the Geico lizard and the cavemen. Oh, and the "I'm a Mac, I'm a PC" commercials are hilarious, too. These ads cost hundreds of thousands of dollars to make and tens of millions of dollars to place on every available channel at every available time so that you won't miss them. Your local ad running once a day during the five o'clock news on one channel won't have the same impact! Even if the household doesn't have a DVR, they'll get up and check on dinner, let the dog out, or go to the bathroom before seeing what you have to offer. A modest campaign like this will still be $1,000 a month or more.

- **Telemarketing:** Business to business, this can work with the right approach and the right person on the phone. Business to consumer, telemarketing doesn't work. There are some industries where cold calling is a necessity, true, but it's a delicate process and if you're a new business or a new entrepreneur think carefully before you spend time and money calling people who haven't asked you to.

- **Direct Mail:** The cost can be prohibitive on anything but a neighborhood level. Sending out postcards that cost 50–80 cents each to more than a couple thousand households can get expensive considering most businesses only experience a 1–3 percent response rate. For large brands, like Dominos, this makes sense because each store is only trying to reach households nearby and they already have brand recognition. If you're trying to establish your brand, direct mail is probably not going to be effective.
- **E-mail:** If you have an e-mail list of customers and prospects that have opted in to receive information from you, by all means, use it. If, however, you are buying a list of e-mails to send your message to, at least consider some of the downsides. While the cost is low, so is the hit rate. Half or more of all e-mails are now unsolicited. This has caused most individuals and businesses to install anti-spam filters to weed out unnecessary e-mails. Even if you get past the spam filter you'll only have a small portion open the e-mail and an even smaller portion read it. You also risk alienating the potential customer by invading what many see as a private space.

These are a few examples of the difficulties small businesses face trying to get noticed among the over-saturated media markets. Certainly, there are exceptions to every argument made here and some companies continue to see solid levels of return on their investment in advertising. I didn't mention radio because it is the one traditional medium that's actually making a bit of a comeback. Their use of podcasting, adding digital and HD feeds, and their ability to reach highly targeted markets has kept radio a viable advertising venue for small businesses. The bottom line is that social networking can take your reach into the millions and target your company to a specific market. It's less expensive and more effective.

Most small business owners have very little time to allocate to social networking; however, it doesn't take as long as you might think once you get your networks set up. We've included as many time saving tactics as we could find (and test) to maximize your results in social networking while minimizing your time spent. As with anything new, there's a learning curve, so things will take longer at first. Once you have your social networking plan in place, maintaining it should only take few hours a week. If you become addicted, however, completely stop all other forms of marketing, and even change your business model; don't say we didn't warn you.

## Using the 80/20 Rule

The 80/20 rule essentially states that 80 percent of any result comes from 20 percent of the input. Whether you've been formally trained in this method or not, you've surely experienced its effect in your personal and business life. Anyone who has attempted a home improvement project knows that 80 percent of the time involved comes from 20 percent of the work: the start of the project and the end. Furthermore, if you look at your own business, you can probably prove this point from your own experiences.

For example, you most likely get 80 percent of your business from 20 percent of your customers. Similarly, you will find the same trend with complaints—80 percent of your complaints come from 20 percent of your customers! The same holds true for social networking—80 percent of you will only need 20 percent, or three, of the top 15 sites: Facebook, LinkedIn, and Twitter. While we recommend getting on Facebook to create a personal profile, for business

**Quick Fact:** The 80/20 concept was born from an observation in 1906 by Italian economist Vilfredo Pareto. In his observations of money and society, he noticed that 80 percent of the wealth was controlled by 20 percent of the people. This concept has since been expanded to be used by management professionals, efficiency experts, motivational speakers, and more as a way of maximizing results with the minimum amount of effort.

it's much like the other featured sites in this book, it may or may not be helpful depending on your target market. However, LinkedIn and Twitter are top professional sites because they are designed for business networking (LinkedIn) and content communication (Twitter). Although we encourage you to explore the full variety of options offered by the various sites, from creating a video campaign on YouTube to building and managing your reputation with Yelp, if you're only going to try one site for your business, make it LinkedIn. If you can go further and try two, add Twitter.

# Who Should Do The Work?

If you're an entrepreneur with no employees, this may be a simple question to answer. *You*, okay, fine, move on to the next section. If you have a business partner or two, or employees then it's time to think this through. With business partners or multiple employees, pick the person with the desire and the skill set needed for social networking. The co-authors of this book, Starr Hall and Chadd Rosenberg, while owning separate businesses, also have a partnership writing books and creating small business guides and consulting packages.

While Chadd toiled away at his computer researching and compiling site reviews, Starr was out in the world of social networking learning most of the tips and strategies delivered in the book. Partnerships are good. Knowing what your strengths are and letting others handle the tasks that may be your weaknesses will ultimately lead to better results. For a great book on this philosophy check out *The 4-Hour Work Week* by Timothy Ferriss.

If you have employees and want to hand over

> **Tip for Employees:** Consider allowing employees to monitor activity, respond to informational requests, but send you any and all issues where negative emotions could come into play. The point is, decide who is going to do what *before* you join the online conversation.

some or all of the social networking responsibilities to them, do so carefully. I suggest creating a quick and simple one- or two-page social networking policy and procedures sheet/manual. List the things that they can and are expected to do and also include postings and or sites that are not allowed. You may have to revise this document often as you learn the social networking ropes, but for now create some type of guidelines for employees when it comes to posting and company involvement on social networks.

# Take Baby Steps

you can run, you must learn to walk. Walk a little in the social networking world and take baby steps. You don't need to learn every site today. I don't even know everything about every site and I probably never will, but that's not my goal. My goal is to find the right site(s) for my company and stay active on them. In addition, when I hear about new sites, I browse them quickly to determine if I should add them to my social networking campaign.

## Create a Social Networking Plan

Just as you would with any other activity for your business, you need a plan. Whether it's for your financials or marketing, without a plan you have no map on how to get from where you are to where you want and need to be. The site reviews and case studies in this book will help you determine what sites you need to incorporate into your plan. It may be overwhelming at first; it certainly was for us. However creating a written plan was helpful.

In addition to determining what sites you need to be on and who's going to do the social networking tasks for your company, you need to make sure that you set your goals. You can set your goals by determining your main objective. What is your

23

purpose for being on these sites? Do you want to build your e-mail list? Brand credibility? Market reach? Test a new market? As you begin to browse sites, check out the site reviews carefully to determine which ones reach your target market. Decide whether you'll focus your attention locally, nationally, or internationally. Are you looking primarily for new customers, strategic partnerships, suppliers, or financiers, or are you trying to build your reputation in your industry?

## Milestones

In putting your plan together you'll certainly want to know how you know when you're successful. Create milestones to help you monitor and quantify your progress. This may be something like: Expand my e-mail list by 10,000 within three months. Or maybe it's: Book 10 paid speaking engagements around the world within six months. These will likely change as you gain more experience; however, you have to know when you're hitting the goals and milestones that you've set; otherwise, what are you social networking for?

## Target Market

If you already know who your target market is, that's great. However, is it the same online and, if so, what sites are they on? On the other side of that, if you don't know who your target market is, you need to find that out before you try to be everything to everyone and waste a lot of time and money. I hear so many companies say, "My products and services are for everyone," often relying on the cliché "Five-year-olds to grandmothers love our … (insert product)." While this may be true, you'll become more profitable if you can niche and narrow your target market and focus.

Try to identify the similar characteristics of your best customers. Quantify their age, where they live, when and where they buy, how much they spend on a typical purchase, anything that's consistent across the "best" group. This process will help you determine which site or sites to work with and also focus where you place your energy once you're on the site. There are tons of articles and resources available online if you do a couple Google searches on "target markets" or "find your target market."

# Building Trust

From 1945 until around 2000 we experienced an era of economic growth and progress unlike any other in history. New products hit the market each year and old ones were forced to improve or face the consequences of a fickle public. Advertisers were keen to take advantage of new technology such as TV to broadcast glamorous images of the next thing we absolutely needed to improve our lives. There were so many brands, so many options, that the buying habits trended toward price, convenience, and of course, "newness." Then little by little, or scandal by scandal, things began to change. All those cheap toys from China turned out to be toxic. The cheap food from Mexico was tainted. The heads of large companies were corrupt. The FDA was inept; e-mail, filled with spam and viruses. Butter gives you heart attacks; margarine is worse.

If you ever watched the news it seemed as though everything and everyone was either bad for you or out to get you. This is what made consumers so skeptical. They lost trust in brands and industries. Ask yourself this question: Are you honest with your customers? Do you truly believe your products or services can and will help people and businesses? Are your ads and marketing materials filled with actual information or just hype and doublespeak? Is your website a resource or is it a sales pitch about how wonderful your products and services are? Where are the credibility or testimonials on your site?

Luckily, social networks provide a place to build trust with potential customers by allowing two-way conversations that are impossible with traditional advertising methods. Giving advice, offering free tips, getting referrals, and participating in—you guessed it—groups builds trust organically. Being the best, the cheapest, or the most convenient isn't going to get you the results you're after. Don't promote these virtues on social networks. Kindness, honesty, and generosity will get you a lot farther.

Now don't get me wrong, I'm not saying that you need to give away your products and services. Although it's healthy to offer your expertise and time to potential clients and customers online as this is how you build trust and relationships. It becomes dangerous to not only your business but also your bank account when you don't set boundaries. This is the biggest mistake I see with online social networking. People fall into

### Top Five Tips That You Must Know When Social Networking

1. Dedicate a set amount of time weekly to social networking. Ideally, make it the same time(s) each week. Set a timer, if you have to, to avoid going over.

2. If you can split the time into two or more events, all the better. Set one time for creating content and posting. Set a separate time for replying to posts and sending social networking-derived e-mails.

3. Use the site reviews to determine what site(s) fit your specific goals. It's not important that you're on multiple sites, just that you're on the right sites for your business. If that's only one site, then it's better to devote all your available time to that one site than spreading yourself too thin among several sites. Think quality over quantity.

4. Most sites will only require weekly updates and posts to keep you current. Microblogs should be attended to daily if possible. Five minutes in the morning, five at lunch, and five at the end of the day will make you look like a social networking champ without putting in too much time.

5. Automate and duplicate. Look for tools (see the case studies) that will allow you to post in one place and have it pushed out to other outlets. If you have to do it manually, copy and paste your thoughts in all available outlets, rather than creating separate content for each.

what I call *panic marketing mode* and they keep giving and giving, asking for nothing in return.

Here are a few quick tips to help you balance your free offers and time giveaways and asking for the business. I call it the 3/3 Rule: *Give away advice and or tips when directly approached no more/no less than three times before you ask for the business.*

Don't spend more than three minutes responding or chatting per person or group.

*Just ask.* This is the one thing that separates the good from the great, the broke from the prosperous: *Asking.* Now don't get me wrong. There's a *big* difference between desperate and sincere. Make sure that you really want the relationship and or the business and that you're not just asking for the sake of getting another deal. Consumers are smart and they can tell the difference between the two!

# How to Communicate on Social Networks

One of the key success tips is to keep your social networking sites and posts current. Whether that's to 20 vendor connections online that you deal with on a regular basis, or 2,000 followers on Twitter that you've never met, you must keep your posts current. Let them know about new products or services you're now offering, sure, but make sure you do more than that. Share content links, tips, and resources. Let them know about a great deal that you found at a supplier. Post a link to an article you read forecasting your industry for the next year. You can also mix it up and share the fact that your son just got an "A" in science—these types of posts make it personable. Another great thing to post is letting your connections know about a good or bad experience with a national brand or better yet, share a great new book you just bought on social networking for business!

So what's the point to all this posting? It's not only to build relationships and connections but to build your company brand name recognition among your markets. Since it takes three times longer and as much money and time to acquire new customers as compared to retaining an existing one, it's crucial that you communicate consistently with your customer base. The idea of a newsletter is old and tired, so keeping the content you provide fresh and engaging is your next challenge. Creating good content is always hard but with social media platforms like podcasts, blogs, and social networks the delivery has never been easier.

## Content and Links

So, what type of content and links should you post on social networks? Nowadays it's a lot easier. Anyone with a webcam can make a video to be viewed by the entire world. The same is true for anyone with a computer and internet connection; they can now publish articles of their own. Think about this: If you had a local or regional columnist come to your business for an interview, how would you prepare? What content would you provide? What if the host of a popular radio show became one of your customers? When doing business through social networking you must assume that every single person you interact with is one of these media VIPs. Each social networker has the ability to post video, audio, or text of their opinions to their network which will likely number into the thousands if they're active.

A single post about your business could easily reach millions of people in a short time without your granting permission, or possibly even knowing who the original author is. The phrase "everyone's a critic" rings true in social networking. This is not to say that you should act out of fear. Be kind, open, honest, and respectful, and let the reviews take care of themselves. By the way, it never hurts to ask for a good review from a happy customer. Several credible, positive reviews can minimize the occasional bad one.

Part of succeeding in this new world is operating with transparency. This means complete open-book honesty, no spin or doublespeak. Before e-mail, cell phones, and social networking, covering up and making excuses was easy. "Sorry, my secretary didn't give me the message" or "I must have accidentally erased it off my machine." Sorry, that's not going to work anymore. Even if you delete a message it stays in the deleted messages folder or the trash. Many services send you an e-mail each time you get a voice mail. Before the internet if you told your customers that a particular item was going to cost extra because you had to ship the materials from across the country but you actually had a supplier in town, how would they know? If you subcontracted work to another company to make large profits, who would find out? Today, if it can be found out, it will be found out. If it's determined you were hiding it, look out.

It's far better to act transparently and let people make their own decisions on whether to do business with you. Announce your strategic partnerships, employ fair and honest pricing models, etc. If you forget to reply to an important call or e-mail, for goodness sakes, just apologize!

# Jump Start Your Social Networking With Top 2 Business Sites

**H**ere's how to get started with *LinkedIn*. You have probably heard the famous saying, "It's not what you know, but who you know" when it comes to building a successful network and business. LinkedIn provides an easy framework and set of tools to broaden your network of customers, vendors, and strategic partners exponentially with a little time and effort. Like most social networks the basic package offering is free. Of course there are premium services and for some of you who advance quickly and make LinkedIn your primary source of new business, these additional features may be worth the minimal cost.

On Linkedin, quality is more important than quantity. LinkedIn's tag line is "Relationships Matter." So how do you not only build the right connections, but build relationships as well?

First you will want to set up your profile completely. We cannot stress enough how important this is. When you look for new connections, the first thing they will do is look at your profile. You wouldn't attend a business mixer without your shoes or shirt, would you? Remember the rules and best practices that apply in our regular "offline" life almost always translate online, as well.

Once you've completed your profile (step-by-step guide included in site review section), you'll want to explore this new world. The best place to start is with the people you already know. LinkedIn allows you to download your contacts from Outlook, Apple Contacts, and a variety of web-based programs into your profile so that you can invite them to join you on LinkedIn and see if anyone you know is already a member. This will provide you with a base of connections from which to grow. It is all right to search through your connections' contacts and check for new potential contacts. You can ask your connection for an introduction or go straight to their connection of interest and invite them to connect with you. Since they're only one generation away they will always have one friend or business associate in common with you.

On the contrary, it's not OK to seek connections from second-generation connections. At the second level, you wouldn't have any person connected in common. Unless this person is an open networker, I suggest that you ask for an introduction through another contact or send a simple message that says, "I would like to connect with you for the following reason [insert reason here]. If you're not an open networker, please *don't* click the "I Don't Know" button, simply archive my email. Thank you for your time and consideration."

The fastest and most effective way to make quality connections is by joining groups in your area of interest or industry. Currently, with the free service you can join up to 50 groups at one time. Each group is a niche or micro community within LinkedIn that shares a common interest or business sector. For example we, as authors and small business coaches, connect with author groups, publishers, meeting planners, small business organizations, entrepreneur networks, business startup groups, or women in business groups. To find these groups you go to the group directory and find a group by keyword(s).

There will usually be a number of groups on each topic so you'll want to be selective about which one you join. I always check the number of members in a group. If there are only 15 members in a group, I usually pass over it and join groups that have thousands of members to increase my network reach.

Once you find the group(s) you want to join, simply ask to join. It's a one-click process but you must be approved by the group administrator. Normally, groups are open and you'll always be welcome but you may run into closed groups that only want people from a narrow sector or level of experience.

Once you're in a group or groups it's important that you start posting. Now, this doesn't mean you should post the first day you're there. In fact, we recommend that you watch the posts for a few days at least to see what people are talking about and what type of content generates the most interest. We did a test in several groups that we joined. In one set of groups we posted what would be considered by most to be a sales pitch for our products and services. In the other set of groups we posted the same information but reformatted it to foster further discussion rather than sales. The results weren't surprising. Not only was the sales pitch ineffective in generating inquiries, but it actually resulted in several complaints!

Meanwhile the discussion posts generated dozens of new business leads.

The point is, you need to offer your knowledge, advice, even your opinion, but not your products and services. People will go to your LinkedIn profile and your website to check you out; if they like what they see, they'll contact you. No one is naive about why you joined a site like LinkedIn. Everyone there is looking to enhance their careers or businesses. The goal then is to get people to interact with you. Give, give, give, and you'll receive your just rewards.

# A Real-Life Example

This book started life as an online toolkit with just the information in the site reviews. It didn't contain either the chapters at the front of the book or the case studies at the end. In a similar fashion we offer toolkits on a variety of subjects including public relations for small businesses, how to become a paid public speaker, and how to become an expert in your field. The Social Networking Toolkit was originally packaged with the PR Toolkit. Now that the PR Toolkit is selling on its own we wanted to generate new interest and, hopefully, sales. Co-author Starr Hall placed two posts on this subject in several groups.

The first post said, "Hi my name is Starr Hall, international PR expert, public speaker, and author. I have a new PR Toolkit that shows you everything a small business needs to design and operate their own PR campaigns without the cost of hiring a PR agency. Please visit www.starrhall.com for details." Now on the surface there doesn't seem to be anything wrong with that post. It's simple, clear, to the point, and merely invites people to go to the website if they'd like more details. As a sales pitch it's pretty light-handed, and yet, it has two critical flaws. One, it doesn't give the reader new information or insight other than the product offering. Two, it doesn't engage the reader to think, act, or continue the conversation. "Please visit (my) website" isn't a call to action.

**Quick Fact:** *A-list media* can be any magazine, newspaper, television show, news program, radio show, and now blogs or websites that have national and international reach.

The second post said, "Hey everyone, I wanted to share with you my top five tips for getting your business A-list media placements: 1) Tip ..." Then at the end of the list it said, "Please share your tips and ideas."

People quickly began posting their suggestions on how to get media placements and feedback to the post. Since Starr is, in fact, a PR expert with tons of experience getting A-list placements for clients, most responders gravitated to her tips over the others posted. Pretty soon, several people began following up by checking out Starr's LinkedIn profile, her website, starrhall.com, and finally contacting her regarding available products and services.

Now think about this for a second. She took five minutes to write the post and another five minutes to copy and paste the post into several groups. That's 10 minutes that generated dozens of new business leads. This was part of our experiment so if she had posted in all 38 groups that she's a member of, instead of half, the response would have been much higher. If only a few of those leads purchased the PR Toolkit that would yield hundreds of dollars, and if even one becomes a client it could result in thousands of dollars of new business.

## What Did We Learn?

The moral of this story is twofold. You must be smart about what you post to achieve the best results and you must post as often as you can. Most of us feel that our lives are already too busy. It's hard to argue, however, that you don't have 10 minutes a week to spare, given the potential of this powerful communication tool. It's okay to post the same content in several groups. Just add a quick note that says, "Posted in other discussion forums" so that the reader knows it's a mass post.

Now that your profile is complete, you've joined as many relevant groups as you can find, and you're posting content regularly; it's time to learn the next LinkedIn tool: *My Q and A*. This function is great way to find connections and build credibility. Here you can ask questions like, "What is the best webinar service company for small business? I'm not too technically savvy and I need something simple and foolproof." In fact, we posted this question and we received answers from people at webinar companies and end-users who had lots of experience with a variety of webinar software. You can ask almost any question you can think of and there is someone out there with the knowledge and experience to help you. Not only will your questions get answered but it'll put you in touch with experts and potential strategic partners from around the world.

The second and arguably more important side of this tool is what happens when you answer questions. LinkedIn has an *Expert Rating*, which can be seen by anyone viewing your profile. The more questions you answer the higher your rating goes. This rating along with individual recommendations that you can request and receive from any of your connections provides an easy way to become a recognized expert in your field. This builds trust, and people buy from others they know and trust. LinkedIn, and social networking in general, provide a great platform for exponentially increasing the number of people you know. Just as important in that quest is building trust along the way.

If you feel comfortable with the site and the features described so far, then you're ready for some more advanced tools, like applications. LinkedIn is continually adding applications that are tools, software applications, and widgets usually developed by a third party to enhance the LinkedIn experience. Most, if not all, are free to use.

Some examples:

- **Slide Share Presentations:** Allows you to upload Power-Point and other presentations to your profile.
- **Wordpress:** Allows you to sync your Wordpress blog with your Linkedin profile. When you post to your blog, it automatically posts to LinkedIn, as well.
- **Company Buzz:** Allows you to monitor the entire internet for conversations (in blogs, forums, social networking sites, etc.) about your business and brand.

These are a couple of the many applications available. The list is growing every day. We would love to give you more detail, but by the time you read this the current offerings will likely be improved and new applications will be the hot thing. Just explore and try to find what will help you conduct your business more effectively and efficiently.

When you login, whether it's once a day, week, or month, be sure to change your status. This can often lead to more interaction with your connections than anything else you do. It doesn't have to be profound, just tell people what you're working on at that moment. Share small victories or current challenges, but keep it positive. Even if you're having a terrible day, try and phrase it so that it will foster constructive interaction, not only condolences and pity. Whatever you post to your status will be on the home page of every connection you have when they login and view their status network update. These updates are sent to your connections via e-mail daily or weekly, depending on their settings.

This may seem like a lot now, but if you spend a little time with each feature you'll quickly find what works for you. Many people get addicted and spend hours a day on social-networking sites. This is *not* necessary to be effective. You can build your network, customer base, and expert status in 30 minutes a week if you work smart and remember 80 percent of your results will come from 20 percent of your effort. The key is figuring out which 20 percent and focusing your time and energy on those actions that deliver the highest returns.

> **New Business.** An investment of only 15 minutes a day "Twittering" earns co-author Starr Hall 80 percent of her new business prospects! These are people and businesses hiring her or buying her products without any prior contact; their only connection was through this amazing social networking tool. Furthermore, Starr was able to achieve this in the first six weeks of using Twitter. Now that's maximizing the 80/20 rule!

# Getting Started on Twitter

If Linkedin is the first 10 percent of your social networking for business efforts, then the next 10 percent should be focused on

Twitter. As important as LinkedIn is for extending your network, Twitter is becoming the communication device of choice for social networkers. Politicians, TV personalities, journalists, business executives, and more have become the early adopters of Twitter's microblogging platform. As you will see in the case studies, more and more small business owners are now tapping into the wide reach of Twitter, using it for new business development and top-of-mind branding.

Brevity is the name of the game when using Twitter. You must define yourself and your business in a single line and all of your posts must be 140 characters or less. Rather than "friends," on Twitter you have "followers." What do you say in your posts? No long paragraphs or detailed thoughts, just a quick sentence or two about what you're doing, experiencing, or thinking at that moment. To the uninitiated this may sound strange and unproductive but there is a beauty, even an art, to Twitter. The value lies not only in the content but, once again, in the connection it provides.

What kind of connections can you make? On Twitter you follow whomever you like: a senator or congressperson, national television journalist, famous author, or the head of the local PTA. In turn, people will begin to follow you. "Following" someone means you're subscribing to all their live posts. If you're like most people, it may still be difficult to see the appeal of following someone or having them follow you. Why do people do this? In short, these brief posts provide a window into the life and mind of the person posting and from a purely voyeuristic standpoint it's entertaining to feel like you have a relationship with a national figure.

However, more important for our purposes here, there is a real value for the small-businessperson. By following people you genuinely have an interest in you're creating a virtual network with all the other people who have similar interests. They'll see your posts and comments and if they like what they read, they'll follow you. As a follower, they're likely to review your profile and check out your website or blog, which often turns into interest in your products and services. In a quick one-week test of Google analytics www.starrhall .com received more referrals from Twitter than any other exterior site. None of the other top sites (Google, Facebook, Linked-In) generated even half the number of hits that Twitter did! With this in mind, here are the top three things you need to do to ensure your Twitter profile is up to snuff.

> **Quick Fact:** There's an option in Twitter to make your updates private. While this may seem like a good thing to do, we recommend leaving your updates open to the public. Anything that helps your followers learn more about you and keep you at the forefront of their minds is a good thing. If you're a private person, Twitter may not be right for you as a business tool.

First, fill in your "one line bio." Take your time and get it right the first time. Remember you never get a second chance to make a first impression. Second, add your website and/or blog on your profile page. You want people who are following you to be able to find your business with ease—and they do check! Lastly, include your geographic location. Many businesses are locally based and are not looking to form relationships outside of their region. You could miss out on opportunities from businesses right in your own backyard.

Twitter, like MySpace, allows for customization of your profile page. It's important to take this opportunity to create a profile page in line with your existing website and branding. Your website developer or graphic designer should be able to provide you with the correct web color codes if you don't already know them. The most important graphic item is your company logo. There's no excuse not to have your logo featured on your Twitter profile. I also suggest that you have your personal photo as your Twitter photo; people love the personal connection "face to face" via Twitter.

Once your profile is complete the actual business of Twittering is simple. There are only three basic actions: finding people you want to follow, following them, and posting your own thoughts and content. The only confusing part might be the language of Twitter. A post or an update is called a Tweet and when you respond to someone's post you Tweet them. "I was twittering about ..." or "I twittered about ..." Silly, yes, but these terms are quickly becoming part of the business vernacular. Even newscasters will say "We want to hear from you, so tweet me at ..."

Building the list of people you follow requires you to search by geography, industry, name, or other keywords. When you find someone of interest, you follow them, that's it. In turn, as you begin to post content, people will start following you.

There are three types of post that we recommend to maintain proper Netiquette (etiquette on the net).

1. **A personal tweet.** This can be something like "Gotta get this Monday rolling, better make it a double at Starbucks!" or "Taking the dog for a walk gives you great perspective on enjoying the little things." Your tweets don't have to be profound or humorous, although it's great if they are. Don't try to be someone you're not. Just be you, and tell the world what you're thinking or doing or reading or whatever! You might be wondering how this will build your business, so let me give you an example. Co-author Starr Hall was in the kitchen hanging out with her youngest son dipping granola bars in chocolate. While checking a couple of e-mails on her Blackberry, she twittered, "just dipped a granola bar in chocolate, mmm ... had to be done." Soon, she was receiving replies from people she didn't know with suggestions of other things you could dip in chocolate (one recommended bacon!). Many of those same people viewed her Twitter profile and several went on to check out her website. The fact is that building relationships over the cold world of texting,

tweets, and e-mails requires that you offer a bit of yourself unscripted, unrehearsed, and (within reason) unfiltered.

> **Quick Fact:** Due to the 140-character limit on Twitter, you may need to tiny any URL links that you post. You do this by going to www.tiny.cc and pasting your URL. This site will make it tiny for you to post on twitter. For example: Take starrhall. com/marketingbootcamp and go to tiny.cc. It will automatically generate a tiny link such as www.tiny078ght.

2. **Industry content and links.** These are posts that usually will fall under your area of expertise. Many people get stuck on what they could offer, especially given the constraint of 140 characters. This is why the link to more information is so important. For example, I posted, "30 Social Networking Terms That You Must Know" with a link to the article on Forbes.com where the information came from. For those of you who think no one wants to read what you have to say, there is your secret weapon. Post about things that you know and are related to your industry, but don't limit yourself to your own brain. There's a lot of great content out there. When you find something that interests you, share it. Once people reply to your post, you can easily add your 2 cents, as well. If someone really likes the content you post, even if it's not your own, they will re-tweet it, meaning they'll post/forward your tweet to their list of followers. This can exponentially increase the number of people who follow you.

3. **Post news or current events.** Again, if it's interesting or provocative to you, then it probably will be for others, too. Adding your own comment to a news event is sure to start conversations. "Dow down another 200 points today. Wondering if we are near the bottom of the curve. Is it time to jump in again?" You will be amazed at whom you'll meet and how your reach will expand with these types of tweets.

## Top 5 Ways to Build Your Following

1. **Search on Twitter:** At the bottom of your Twitter profile page there's a "search" link. When clicked it will take you to a new page labeled "Search by Twitter." On that screen look for the "Advanced Search" option. From the advanced search page you'll be able to look for people within a specific set of parameters to make sure you're only connecting with people who serve a purpose for you or your business. Remember the way to get followers is to follow others; especially those with large numbers of followers!

2. **Import contacts:** In your Twitter profile there's a link "Find on other networks." This will let you upload contacts from a variety of mail programs including gmail, Yahoo!, AOL, hotmail, and MSN. Other popular mail programs like Outlook and Apple Mail aren't supported at the time of this writing but should be soon. Until then an easy work-around is to set up a gmail account, import your Outlook or Apple Mail contacts, then re-import them on Twitter. As with LinkedIn, starting with the people you already know can give you a jump start on finding and connecting with new people.

3. **Follow suggested users:** Twitter provides a section called "Suggested Users" which will give you a list of whom Twitter thinks you should connect with based on similarities in profile. Check these each time you log in to get a fresh batch of people whom you can follow and in turn follow you. You can easily add 20–30 followers each time you do.

4. **TwitterGrader.com:** Twitter Grader is an external site that gives you a Twitter grade or rank based on the total reach and the number of followers you have. From your rank, number of followers and keywords in your profile Twitter Grader can also produce a list of folks you should follow. This will also typically generate 20–30 connections for each use.

5. **Twinfluence.com:** Twinfluence provides a "Top 50" Twitterers in three categories: reach, velocity, and social capital. Your reach on Twitter is determined by the number of followers (also know as first-order followers) plus the number their followers (or second-order followers). So for example, if you had five followers and each of your followers had five followers your total reach would be 30.

Velocity is the average number of first- and second-order followers you've accumulated since establishing your Twitter account. If reach determines your influence then velocity determines the rate your acquire influence. Social capital refers to the average number of followers your followers possess. You may never make it onto one of these lists or use these terms at your next cocktail party, but you should consider following some if not all of the top users ranked on Twinfluence. Not only will you add hundreds of followers but many of those followers will have thousands of followers of their own. Within two months of joining Twitter co-author Starr Hall was able to achieve a reach of 4.2 million using all of these techniques combined.

## Twitter Lingo

- **@ (at) replies:** @ replies are a way to send a public tweet to one individual. For instance, if you were to send a message directly to  Starr Hall (username starrhall), you would begin your post with @starrhall. This is primarily used when sending a reply to a tweet. Remember that your followers can see these posts even though you're directing it to starrhall; it's not private.
- **Retweet:** Since a post is called a tweet any reposting or forward is called a retweet. When a Twitterer sees a post they think their followers would like, they repost the content (with credit, of course) to their followers. When people retweet your content it expands your reach, likewise you can expand the reach of any twitterer by retweeting their content. Do this often as people appreciate it and are likely

to repay the favor. To retweet, enter RT or retweet at the beginning of your post followed by the original author's username; then add the content from the original tweet.

- **Direct message:** AKA DM—a direct message is a private way to send a message from one user to another without it being posted to other followers. Like any e-mail communications it's important that you're careful when replying to any unsolicited message. There are a number of phishing attacks that use direct messages on Twitter to get you to view a link or sign in to your Twitter account only to steal your username and password or take you to a website containing malware.

Managing the world of Twitter can be cumbersome once your number of followers gets into the hundreds or thousands. TweetDeck (tweetdeck.com) is a free software program, known as a Twitter client, it takes all the Twitter feeds and creates easy-to-follow user-controlled columns of bite-sized data. Without going into detail on how this works, just know that with this software you can reduce what would take two to three hours to sort through down to 15 to 30 minutes. Now that's using the 80/20 rule to maximize your social networking experience!

# Blogging 101

 *blog*, also known as a *weblog*, is a type of website usually maintained by an individual with regular entries that include content articles, tips, posts of commentary, description of events, or other material such as photos, graphics, or video. Most blogs are used to provide valuable content specific to a certain topic or area of interest from the author.

Blog entries are commonly displayed in reverse-chronological order, although some blog hosts now allow the option to change this. A blog can be business-related or some are personal, what I like to call online diaries. A typical blog combines text, images, and links to other blogs, web pages, media links related to the topic, videos, and photos. The ability for readers to leave comments in an interactive format is an important part of many blogs.

Most blogs are text-based, although some focus on photographs (photoblog), art (artlog), videos (vlog), music (MP3 blog), and audio (podcasting). Micro-blogging, which allows you to type very short posts, has been surfacing over the past few years. Twitter is a great example of a successful microblog. Most blogs can be searched and tracked through a site called

*Technorati.* This site is a blog search engine and recently reported tracking more than 110 million blogs.

# Blogs and Your Business

So, how does a blog help you build your business? Blogs can be very effective in building your business and connections online if you follow a few simple steps. First of all, before you even start a blog, you need to determine if blogging is right for you. Just because there are a lot of blogs on the net doesn't mean this will be the best tool for you in building your business and network. Blogging is a commitment, and if you're going to be successful at blogging, you really should have a basic knowledge of surfing the internet and actual enjoy doing it. You will need to read, research, and surf the net to find valuable content, case studies, and statistics all related to your topic or area of blog interest.

If writing does not come naturally to you, there is another option you can use to post content on your blog. I suggest researching other valuable content that is not direct from a competitor and include it in your blog posts. If you do this, you must make sure that you get permission to use the content and give the proper credit as well as link back to the content site if necessary or requested. I have found that writing your own personal posts, tips, and content are the most powerful, and I often will use an article or statistic to back up my post.

## How Often?

How often you should post to your blog is entirely up to you and your commitment. If you are a basic user, I suggest at least two posts per month. I strive to post one per week. I've found that the more I post, the more I am able to capture opt-in emails for my database. I receive more e-mail from potential clients than I am able to engage in conversation with, and my client and product sales conversion rate is higher. Serious bloggers who work at it full time post daily—some even most multiple times throughout the day.

# Reasons for Blogging

Once you've decided that you can commit to blogging, you need to know why blogging is used. There are many reasons why individuals and businesses are starting to use this media tool to build their business. Here are the top five:

1. To establish yourself as an expert in your industry or area of interest.
2. To connect with people who have similar interests and/or stay connected.
3. To make a difference.
4. To market or promote something.
5. As an additional revenue stream.

What is your reason or goal for blogging? You need to determine how you want to use your blog before you go live on the internet. Your blog has a better chance of succeeding if you know from the beginning what you hope to accomplish with it. Are you trying to establish yourself as an expert in your field? Are you trying to promote your business? Are you simply blogging for fun and to share your ideas and opinions? Think about what you would like to gain from your blog in the next three months, one year, and even three years from now. Once you decide this, you can then design your blog and plan to fit these goals.

Your blog's design and content should reach out to your target market. For example, if your intended audience or target market is the music industry, the design and content would be quite different from a blog targeted at executives. Your blog visitors can be turned off by design that does not pull them emotionally. In order to avoid losing your audience, make sure your design is consistent with your profession and the image you wish to project.

It's also important to have graphic design and copy balance. Remember that your blog is a brand that represents a specific message and image to your audience. It's important that you stay consistent with your imagery and copy. Do not have more of one than the other; this will help you gain reader loyalty.

Aside from being consistent with your blog design and layout, it is equally important to be persistent. If you are persistent, your blog will begin to build and become very busy. A blog that is not updated frequently might be perceived as static web pages. The usefulness of blogs comes from their timeliness and constant interactions. While it's important not to publish meaningless posts, it's essential that you update your blog frequently. The best way to keep readers coming back is to always have something new and valuable for them to see and use. Adding tips and resources in posts are an excellent way to keep your readers happy.

It's essential that your blog welcomes readers and invites them to join a two-way conversation. Ask your readers to leave comments posing questions. Then respond promptly to comments from your readers. Doing so will show that you value them, and it will keep the conversation going. Continue the conversation by leaving comments on other blogs, inviting new readers to visit your blog for more lively discussions. Your blog's success is partially dependent on your readers' loyalty to it.

## Marketing Your Blog

How are you going to get readers if you don't market your blog? Much of your blog's success relies on your efforts outside your blog. Those efforts include finding like-minded bloggers and commenting on their blogs, participating in social bookmarking sites such as Digg and StumbleUpon, as well as joining social networking sites such as Facebook, LinkedIn, and Twitter. The old saying "If you build it, they will come" does not ring true with blogging. You must develop a successful blog by creating compelling content as well as working outside of your blog to promote and develop a community around it. When you post on other social sites and networks, again make it about the audience and the reader, not about you. Ask them to post questions or comments.

Something that will set you apart from most blog sites is to take risks. Don't be afraid to try new things on your blog. Maybe it's adding a new plug-in to posting a free downloadable report. It's

**Tip:** When you post are posting about your blog on social sites, tiny the URL by going to www.tiny.cc so that the link does not look like a personal sales push back to your site.

**Example:** Check out the top five tips on social networking, click here: www.tinyurl5678.com.

important that you keep your blog fresh by implementing changes that will enhance it. On the other hand, don't fall for uploading every new bell and whistle that becomes available for your blog. Instead, take some time to review each option and determine how it will help you reach the goals you have for your blog and how your audience will respond to it. If you're not sure, just ask your audience.

Like social networking, blogging is an ever-changing place, and no one knows everything there is to know about blogging. Experienced bloggers are part of a close-knit community, and the majority of bloggers understand that everyone is a beginner at some point. In fact, bloggers are some of the most approachable and helpful people you can find. Don't be afraid to reach out to fellow bloggers for help. The success of the blogosphere relies on networking, and most bloggers are always willing to expand their networks regardless of whether you're a beginning blogger or seasoned pro. Don't be afraid to ask.

Beyond all the advice, resources, and how-to information in this book, you must remember to be yourself. Your blog is an extension of you and your brand, and your loyal readers will keep coming back to hear what you have to say. Inject your personality into your blog and adapt a consistent tone for your posts. Determine whether your blog and brand will be more effective with a comical tone, a professional tone, or a snarky one. Stay consistent with that tone in all of your blog communications. People don't just read blogs to get the news; they can read a newspaper for that. Instead, they read blogs to be entertained and to get bloggers' tips, resources, and opinions on the news, the world, life, family, and more. Unless you are a reporter, don't blog like one. You need to blog like you're having a conversation with each of your readers. More importantly, speak and blog from the heart.

# Making Money with Your Blog

Now that you know if you want to blog, how to get your blog set up, and how to market it, you might want to know a few ways on how to make money with your blog. Although blogs are great for building credibility, connections, and e-mail lists, they are also an excellent way to make money if executed properly.

Including advertisements on your blog is the most obvious way to derive an income from your blogging efforts. Ads can come in the form of text links or banner ads, and advertising options are available that you can easily tap into through pay-per-click, pay-per-post, and affiliate programs online. Amazon Associates, Google AdSense, eBay Affiliates, and Pay-Per-Post are just a few of the most common advertising programs available to bloggers. There are plenty of resources on the internet to help you find the best advertising tools for your blog. Your blog host might have suggestions for you as well.

Another simple way to monetize your blog is by selling merchandise through a service such as CafePress, which will work with you to create custom items for you to sell through your blog. Or you can create your own products, books, and CDs and have them available on your site. All you need to do is include the link on your blog.

Although I've seen many bloggers make money by reviewing products, events, and businesses through blog posts, most of these bloggers have established respected credentials in their area or industry. If you're already an established expert in your field, then this is a great way to earn additional revenue. If you're working on establishing your credibility and expertise, then I suggest that you put together an e-book and offer it for sale through your blog. Make sure that your e-books have valuable information and are not just e-book sales pitches. You will lose credibility and readers. I often offer new e-book releases as additional information or exclusive information just for readers of my blog.

I have also worked with a lot of bloggers who add a donation button to their blogs, asking readers to make a monetary donation to keep the blog alive. Donations are also solicited with clever taglines such as, "If you like this blog, why not buy me a drink or a cup of coffee?" The donation link leads the reader to another website shopping cart such as Paypal, where the individual can easily make their donation.

## Choosing a Blog Host or Platform

There are many blog hosts and platforms to choose from. You need to first determine what your budget is because blog platforms come with a variety of price points ranging from free to a variety of pricing options. There are three main things that you might pay for:

1. The blog platform itself
2. Hosting for your blog
3. Domain name

Different blogging platforms offer different levels of service. Some like Blogger.com and Wordpress.com offer both the platform, domain name, and hosting for free. Others like WordPress.org (note this is different to WordPress.com) offer the platform for free but you then need to find and pay for your own hosting and domain name. Other costs you might like to factor in at an early stage include:

**Design.** All platforms come with free templates (some more professional looking than others), but if you want a more individual look, you'll either need to have some design skills, know someone who does, or be willing to pay for a design.

**Blog tools/metrics.** There are any number of tools you can pay for to help you in your blogging. These might include stats packages, for example. Although you can get free ones, you can also pay for more features, such as offline blog posting tools and so on. In the beginning you might not need any of these, however down the road and into your blogging success future, you will find them useful.

If you haven't had any experience in creating a blog or website before and are not a technologically-minded person, then there are some blog platforms and set-ups that will be much more suited to your needs if you know a few of the basics, or are at least willing to learn them.

The other option of course is to find someone who is tech savvy to help you out (either paid, as a friend, or even a trade). One of the great things about blogging and being online is that there is an entire community including forums and groups dedicated to helping people get the most out of their chosen platforms.

Over the last few years different platforms have come and gone, and I suspect they will in the years ahead, as well. What you need to decide is if you are going to have a hosted blog versus a standalone platform.

## Hosted Blog Platforms

This is what many beginning bloggers start out doing simply because they are easy and usually quite cheap, if not free. The most popular of these systems are Blogger.com or Wordpress.com. TypePad.com also runs hosted blogs, although they do offer a standalone option through remote hosting.

These blogs are "hosted" blog platforms because the site such as WordPress.com "hosts" your blog on their domain. After what is usually a pretty easy set-up process, they will give you a web address (URL) that will be a combination of their own URL and the name of your blog.

## A Few Pros and Cons of Hosted Blog Platforms

### Pros:

- **Cheap or free to run.** Most hosted options are free.
- **Relatively easy to set up.** Most of these types of blogs can be set up with a basic default template within minutes by filling in a few fields with your options and choosing a template design.
- **Simple to run.** Posting is as simple as filling in a few fields and hitting publish.
- **Updates automatically.** If the blog platform updates, it will automatically do so for you.
- **Indexed in search engines quickly.** One of the advantages of many hosted blog platforms is that they are put onto domains that have good page ranks already.

### Cons:

- **Less configurable.** One of the biggest frustrations with hosted blog owners is their limited options for customization. This varies from platform to platform within the hosted options. For example, WordPress.com has quite limited design options. You can't add ads to templates, making it a poor choice to make money with. Blogger.com doesn't give the option for categories, and TypePad has different options depending on which level you buy in at.
- **Default design limitations.** Your blog might end up looking similar to other blogs on the net. This is because the default templates get used over and over, and if you're a beginner they can be difficult to adapt. For instance with Blogger.com as with several other platforms, to make changes, you need to know CSS and HTML to edit your templates.
- **Generic URL.** Having your own URL can give a sense of professionalism and memorability to a blog that hosted options might well go without. While there are some very successful blogs on hosted platforms, some bloggers believe that having your own URL is more professional if you are using your blog for business purposes.

## Standalone Blog Platforms

The other type of blog platform is one hosted under your own domain/URL. This is what I do with my blog. It is more professional and brands your URL. My blog is located on my site at www.starrhall.com. Standalone blog platforms that many use include Greymatter, PMachine, TextPattern, and Expression Engine, to name just a few.

### Pros and Cons of Standalone Blog Platforms

**Pros:**

- **Full control of design.** Standalone blogs are generally very adaptable. If you know someone who's savvy with HTML or CSS, this option is great for you. If you're the techie, better yet! This way you can create unique and clever designs.
- **Free platforms.** While you end up paying for your domain name and hosting, systems like these are usually free to run. Some have license fees if you're having multiple blogs or using them for commercial purposes, but many are open source.
- **URL.** Having your own domain name is great for many reasons. First, it's easier to remember, and second, it's more professional and brandable.

**Cons:**

- **Complicated set up.** Once again this depends upon your technical abilities. When you move to a standalone platform, the complexity of set-up tends to increase. There are good tutorials around for most of the platforms to help with this process, but for many it is daunting. I suggest outsourcing it to a professional. I've found set-up to range between $100 to $500 for one blog, For me it's worth it. You can also find a web host that will install your web platform for you. This is becoming increasingly popular.
- **Updates.** If a blog platform changes or up-dates a version, updating from one to another can be complicated if you don't know what you're doing.

# Proper Net-i-quette

**H**aving the proper net-i-quette is crucial to your online success and in building your network. The same rules apply online as they do offline: if you can't say something nice, don't say anything at all, and don't post something that you wouldn't say in person. It is not healthy nor is it in anyone's best interest to be confrontational online.

It is imperative that you are very careful about what you post. If someone responds to your post with a negative comment or they argue your point, stay calm and respond politely and professionally. I have had this happen a few times and because of my response, the other person ended up looking foolish, and I came out as the professional that I am. Being right is one thing, but being right and loud about it is not the best approach. It is certainly not worth jeopardizing your online reputation to respond in the negative. Although some replies are necessary to maintain your reputation, you still need to be cautious as to how you post your response. If you aren't sure, ask a co-worker, colleague, or a friend to read before you post back.

Think about social net-i-quette this way, would you do the following in person or face-to-face?

- Immediately assume that you are friends without properly introducing yourself?
- Consistently talk about or promote yourself without even listening to the other person?
- Randomly approach someone that you barely talk to and repeatedly ask for favors?

If you answered yes to any of these questions, you may need a refresher course on proper etiquette for in-person networking, as well on social media. I have included a few top Social Networking no-nos for top sites. Avoid these and learn how to manage and maintain online relationships on a variety of popular social media sites.

# Facebook

- Adding users as friends without proper introductions. If you don't already have a relationship with someone you'd like to make friends with, introduce yourself and tell why you'd like to connect with him or her.
- Abusing application invites and consistently inviting connections to participate in mafia games and quizzes. This is considered spam.
- Posting your logo as your profile photo. Facebook is about personal connection.
- Abusing group invites. If your friends are interested, they'll likely join without your "encouragement." And if they don't accept, don't send the group request more than once by asking them to join via e-mail, wall post, or Facebook message. It's annoying and again could be considered spam.
- Not using your real name on your profile. People you don't know won't add you to their friends list if you're not honest about who you are.

- Publicizing a private conversation on a wall post. Facebook wall posts are public to all your friends, even one-on-one wall post. Private matters should be handled via e-mail or Facebook private messages.

> **Facebook side note:** Some individuals aren't open networkers, and they won't accept your invite or connection even with the proper introduction on a personal site such as Facebook. If you're looking to establish a professional relationship with someone, consider LinkedIn.

- Tagging individuals in unflattering pictures that could damage your friend's reputation. In addition, if your friends request to be untagged, don't make a stink of it.

## Twitter

- Following a user and then unfollowing them before they have a chance to follow back or unfollowing them as soon as they follow you.
- Consistently using your tweets for nothing but self-promotion.
- Doing a mass-follow so that you can artificially inflate your numbers, then use that number as a success metric for influence.
- Asking your followers to retweet your Tweets on a consistent basis. If your content is valuable and of interest, it will be retweeted. You won't have to ask.
- Only posting your blog's RSS feed on Twitter. It's not all about you and eventually if you keep doing this, people will unfollow you.
- Don't broadcast your dissatisfaction with a Twitterer over Twitter. This is unprofessional. Take it up with the person directly via a direct message.
- Sending auto-direct messages that are really spam to those who follow you. Three days later, you may wonder why they aren't following you anymore.

- If you're engaged in a chat among several people by using the @ sign to directly communicate on the feed, take the conversation private and allow valuable content and posts to take the space, not conversations that have nothing to do with anyone but you and the Twitterers involved.

# LinkedIn

- Asking for an endorsement from individuals you don't know or that you really didn't do business with directly.
- Gathering the e-mail addresses of users you're connected to and using this list to promote your own company or service outside the LinkedIn site. Recipients on your e-mail list should opt in.
- When you join a group, not following the group's posting and discussion rules.
- Not properly introducing yourself to people before you ask them to connect with you.

# Social News Sites

- Submitting only your own articles and posts to social media sites.
- Consistently "taking" (asking for votes) but never giving back. Social news is about reciprocal relationships. Even if the people you're asking votes of will never actually ask you for votes, a random IM that pops up that says "Digg this for me" is far more obtrusive than saying, "hey, how's it going?" and having a real conversation first.
- Shouting out the same story repeatedly to your friends. Once is enough.
- Submitting a story to a social news site that is completely off-topic. It's important to understand the sites that you target. Your story about restaurant reviews does not belong on the fashion social news site no matter how you try to spin it.

# YouTube

- Asking someone repeatedly to watch your crummy video, subscribe to your channel, and give you a 5-star rating.
- Sending more than one video per week to your list or contacts.

# StumbleUpon

- Sending more than one story to your network daily. The key to success is moderation.
- Submitting and reviewing only your own articles.

# Blogging and Commenting

- Using content from another blog without giving credit.
- Sending a pitch to a blogger requesting a link exchange even though your site has no relevancy to their content.
- Arguing or bashing on your blog or in the comment section on someone else's blog.

# Other Social Sites

- Uploading your entire e-mail address book and inviting anyone and everyone to join on the social networking site with you.
- Volunteering your e-mail account's password to other social sites, clients, or partners.
- As an FYI, your e-mail account password should not be the same as the one you use for your social profiles. That's not a question of etiquette, it's common sense!
- Think about the consequences of your engagement on any social site. Racial slurs, criticisms without warrant, and abuse don't work in person, and they especially don't help you online. Consider how your comments would be perceived before you actually post them and leave out your emotions at all times. Anything that you post is public record and can be used against you. Not all blogs will

remove a comment after you've requested that they do so simply because you were angry when you wrote the comment. Before you hit "Post," stop and think about how it will be a permanent reflection of your identity and that it may never be erased. With every post, you're leaving a digital signature and impression. How do you want to be remembered and talked about online?

# How to Be Efficient with Your Social Networking

 **As** if you didn't have enough marketing tasks on your plate, and now you are adding social networking! How are you going to find the time to fit all these new and exciting sites and techniques into your schedule? Over the past few years that I've actively been involved in social networking, I'e found a lot of time-saving tips and tricks that I'll share with you throughout this chapter. All you have to do is read the suggestions and figure out which ones will work best for you and your business.

## Social Networking Clients

Most social sites have what are called "social networking clients." These are additional sites or free downloadable software to enhance or simplify your networking experience on the particular site that the client supports. For example, Tweetdeck is free downloadable software that helps simplify your Twitter experience. It manages all the messages that come directly to you or that involve your Twitter name in the conversation. This way you can respond only to Twitter conversations in which you're being mentioned or directly messaged.

This is only one of the many tools that Tweetdeck offers to support you.

Facebook has clients and partners such as Networkedblog, which allows you to connect your blog to your Facebook. Linkedin has dozens of partners and clients such as SlideShare where you can upload your PowerPoint presentations or slide shows and share them on your Linkedin page. Squidoo offers dozens of partnering clients as well and allows you to connect your Squidoo to YouTube, Linkedin, Facebook, and many more.

## Automated Set-Up

Many social networking sites now offer automated set-up where you can connect your Twitter account to your Facebook page and your Linkedin page to Twitter and so on. This way, you only have to post in one or two places, and it will automatically post to the other sites on which you have set this up. Before you do this, make sure you want your posts to automate. Some people set up personal profiles and have a professional focus on other sites. You don't want to post something that's personal if you're set up on automated, the post would go out to your professional networks as well.

The other thing to consider with social networking automation is that there are different audiences on different sites. Your Facebook page might have more of a personal mix where as your LinkedIn is professional. Your Squidoo or Good Reads profile might be geared toward readers for your new book or ebook report. I only have my Twitter and Facebook linked for automation, along with my blog.

Social networking doesn't need to take a lot of time if you set up your profiles correctly from the beginning, and if you know what sites you need to be on. If you set a schedule and stick to it, your social networking experience and results will be far better than if you post on sites for the sake of being on them. Where people tend to waste a lot of time is when they get caught up in the back and forth and when they don't have a system in place.

# Keeping Things Under Control

You don't need to e-mail back or talk to every single person that responds to your post or that thanks you online for posting something. The easiest way to stay connected yet not get overwhelmed is to only respond to conversations where the person is asking for an answer, further information, or guidance. If they simply post a thank you, let it be. Another effective way to stay on task with social networking is to set up a response system. One or two days a week, set aside 15 to 20 minutes to respond to your social networking e-mails and posts.

If you have e-mails from all the sites you're on coming to your personal or business e-mail address, then set up a file in your e-mail system called "social follow-up." Check this folder on the days you choose for responding, go through them one at a time, and send a quick one-minute response and move on. If the contact is someone with whom you want to do business or stay in touch, then add that person to your "rock star" file. This is a file that you set up in your e-mail or even in your database management program to keep important contacts' information and connection alive.

## Common Mistakes

There are several common mistakes I see with social networking that waste a lot of time and money as well as lose connections and friends or followers. One of the biggest mistakes is people making a sales pitch online. Whether your company is product- or service-related, it doesn't matter. You must build credibility before you start selling. This rule applies whether it's online or in-person networking. You aren't going to walk up to someone at an event and say "check out my consulting services or my product" before you even mention your name or get to know this person, correct? So why would you do that online?

I've already mentioned the second most common mistake in a prior chapter, but I feel it's necessary to repeat it here because it's so important. You need to allocate a certain amount of time to social networking and stick to it. Whether it's going to be 15 minutes a day or two hours, set a timer, be disciplined, and make sure that you stop when the timer goes off. It's easy to get caught up in a conversation or a new site, but you need to walk away or you'll start to get sucked in and controlled by your computer and the internet.

In my beginning days of social networking I spent close to 40 hours a week researching, posting, asking questions, checking out new sites, talking with connections, setting up profiles, and even my blog. At the time there were not a lot of training sites, videos, and tutorials available to make it easier for me. If there had been, I would have spent the money, no questions asked. Nowadays the internet is filled with tips, tutorials, and step-by-step videos. Some are free. Most are not, but it's worth the $20 to $50 for a 20-minute training session. It would take you 40 hours to learn what most of these tutorials will teach you in 20 minutes.

# Reviews of Social Networking Sites

## Social Network Sites
### Facebook (facebook.com)

### What Is It?

A self-described "social utility that connects people with friends and others who work, study and live around them," Facebook lets small-business owners expand their networks, communicate with friends and potential customers, and share business information through blog posts, pictures, and videos. Facebook is a social-networking site that allows users to join networks broken down into categories such as schools, employers, and geographic regions to connect with other Facebook members. Members can update personal profiles to provide information about themselves and post messages for their Facebook friends on their wall. They can also add applications and surveys to their profiles to further share their personalities and preferences.

### Site Stats

**Born:** February 4, 2004
**Users:** More than 200 million active users worldwide
**Demographics:** The fastest-growing Facebook demographic is users age 25 or older. The site claims to maintain 85 percent market share of four-year U.S. universities, though more than half of its users are outside of college
**Cost to join:** Free

### Highs: What the site is good at and for ...

Clean layout leads to easy navigation of profile pages as well as the entire site. One of the site's most popular features, the Photos application, allows users to upload albums and photos. They currently have a per-album limit. The site's News Feed gives users an easy way to keep up with their friends. Since Facebook is organized around networks, it's easy to reconnect with old school friends or work colleagues.

### Lows: What's difficult or missing from the site ...

Privacy issues are Facebook's consistent problem child. There have been past concerns with the difficulty of deleting Facebook accounts, though as of February 2008 users can directly contact the site to request permanent deletion. Other privacy concerns have included the use of the site for surveillance and data mining.

E-mail alerts force users to come back to the website when a user posts to a wall, sends another user a note, or when a group post is received.

Facebook is considered a poor advertising platform, with average click-through rates for ads just 0.04 percent, or 400 clicks for every 1 million views.

### Straight talk: If you're looking for these types of customers you should be on this site ...

- College students
- Internet-savvy users
- Recent college graduates beginning their careers
- The 35-and-up crowd, which as of August 2007 accounts for more than 41 percent of Facebook users.

### Another angle: This site could help grow your business if you're in one of the following categories ...

- Photo or video online sharing media sites: Facebook is particularly strong when it comes to its Photo section
- Seeking to tap into an active community of potential business customers
- Hoping to brand yourself and your services

- Seeking to expand your professional network.

## A Facebook profile consists of ...

**Main picture:** For a small business, using a logo rather than a personal picture may be the way to go. Make sure your logo or picture is clean, easy to see, and sufficiently sized for the space allowed.

**Networks:** Networks differ from groups in that they connect people from the same region, school, or workplace. These networks provide targeted information and connections with people who share one or more of these attributes, giving you a better perspective on target markets. Networks also allow businesses with regional parameters to see and connect with potential customers without having to run filtered searches through millions of Facebook members.

**Groups:** Groups are more focused than networks, but not bound by any network parameters. They offer connections to people and businesses within a particular topic of interest. Participating in Facebook Groups provides direct communication with potential clients and partners who have already opted in to discuss and learn about a given topic. You can also create your own group or send more generic messages to entire groups, as long as these messages are informative and not a direct sales pitch.

**Discussion Boards:** The Discussion Board tackles a specific topic raised by principal members of a given group. All members are welcome to discuss this topic.

**The Wall, Posted Items, and Notes:** The Wall is an unscripted place that allows members to post just about anything, including photos and links to videos. Posted Items provide a way for you to show all your friends a message, photo album, or video. Notes can be posted on your page as well as on a group page if posted to a group. However, these will not be sent automatically to your friends as with posted Items.

**Photos:** Posting photos that better describe you or your business will give visitors a personal sense of you as well as your products and services. You can also post photos whenever you have something to share with the community, Facebook Marketplace is essentially an online classified ads section. Since ads are classifieds by regions, you must belong to at least one network. Though you cannot advertise your business or services through the Marketplace, you can post job listings here.

## Site Add-ons

**Toolbars:** The Firefox toolbar adds Facebook search and activity notifications to Firefox and lets users view friends and share content without visiting Facebook itself. Get the Firefox toolbar here: developers.facebook.com/toolbar. Facebar is another Firefox toolbar for Facebook and offers automatic login, search and quick links. Get Facebar here: https://addons.mozilla.org/en-US/firefox/addon/3855.

**Photo Album Downloader:** One-click downloading of Facebook albums. Get it here: https://addons.mozilla.org/en-US/firefox/addon/4481.

**Boost for Facebook:** Adds a suite of Facebook-specific features to your browser, including skins, notifications, auto-poke, auto-login, friends in your sidebar, and more. Get it here: https://addons. mozilla .org/en-US/firefox/addon/3120.

**Firefox Universal Uploader:** An uploading and downloading tool for many online services, including Facebook. Get it here: https://addons .mozilla.org/en-US/firefox/addon/4724

**Autoslideshow:** Grabs all images from a current page and displays a slideshow of them within Firefox. Works with Facebook and many other photo sites. Get it here: https://addons.mozilla.org/enUS/ firefox/addon/3177.

## Site Customization Resources

Though Facebook offers less profile page customization than other social-networking sites such as MySpace, there are still ways to make your page stand out. Remember to keep your customizations professional and relevant to your business. Here are a few resources:

**All Layed Out:** alllayedout.com. Offers customization resources for many social-networking sites, including Facebook.

**Facebook Expressions:** fbexpressions.com. Free wallpaper designs for Facebook profiles.

**Facebook Applications:** facebook.com/applications. Add any of these thousands of external applications to your Facebook page; just make sure they're relevant to your audience and don't muddy your message.

## Site Marketing and Advertising Opportunities

Social networking lets you promote your business in a number of creative ways. Here are a few ideas to get you started:

**Profile:** Create a compelling real-world story to add context and character to your business and its services.

**Facebook Groups:** Tap into an active community of potential customers.

**Facebook Pages:** Allows businesses to create a brand presence. They're more customizable than Groups, with "fans" invited to join. These are free and a good way to conduct viral marketing.

**Facebook Events:** Get fully featured pages offering all pertinent details. This makes it easy to get the word out to hundreds of people at once, as well as to build a community based on your upcoming event.

**Advertising Tools:** Marketers with a budget can take advantage of Facebook's integrated and self-serve options. For budgets ranging from a few dollars to several hundred thousand, here are a few paid advertising options:

- **Social Ads:** These offer the option to pay on either a CPC or CPM basis and have powerful targeting capabilities. Social Ads are completely self-serve and provide real-time feedback. They also get placements in the News Feed, which increases exposure.
- **Polls:** These are a simple way for marketers to do research in their target audience. Real-time results are streamed to a dashboard that lets you break down results by gender and age.

- **Integrated opportunities:** Marketers with $50,000 or more to spend are encouraged to contact Facebook to explore more integrated advertising opportunities

## Tools for Application Developers

Marketers who are able to harness technical resources may be able to join the thousands of third-party applications already available on Facebook. Third-party applications should be prepared to take advantage of the following for maximum success:

- Profile Box
- Mini Feed
- News Feed
- Invitations
- Facebook Notifications
- E-mail Notifications
- Application Directory

**Market Lodge:** Produced by bSocial Networks Inc., this program pays Facebook members a 10 percent commission on all merchandise or service sales based on their recommendations. Facebook members who use Market Lodge can customize their own stores by selecting from more than 15,000 products sold by hundreds of vendors. Once a member's personal store is created, Facebook users can then invite people from their network to peruse the online stores. Users can also buy from their own stores and qualify for the 10 percent commission. Merchants handle all inventory, order processing, and delivery arrangements.

## Getting Started on Facebook

Follow these steps to launch your own Facebook profile and start expanding your business network:

- On Facebook, enter the requested signup information and click the "Sign Up" button. You'll then be prompted through a security check.
- From here you'll be able to fill in further information about your profile.

- Begin customizing your page and searching for friends. Remember that you won't be able to start working with Facebook until you verify the e-mail address used to register.

---

# MySpace (myspace.com)

## What Is It?

An international site that offers users e-mail, a forum, communities, video, and weblog space, MySpace may be of most direct use to small-business owners catering to the 14- to 25-year-old age range. Those seeking pop culture fans will also benefit from joining the site, as will businesses targeting internet-savvy users. Myspace is the most visited social-networking site on the Internet. Originally developed by Intermix/eUniverse, Inc. and spearheaded by current CEO Chris DeWolfe and current president Tom Anderson (known for being the first friend for all new accounts), the site quickly became popular among teens, young adults, and rock bands. Users create a free account and develop their own profile page to interact with fellow members. These profile pages are remarkably flexible, with options for users of various skills to customize as they wish.

## Site Stats

**Born:** August 15, 2003

**Users:** More than 100 million registered accounts, an estimated 300,000 new users sign up daily

**Demographics:** Weighted toward the 14–25 age range. Currently the site is pushing toward a greater focus on small businesses, approximately 6 million new businesses registered in 2008

**Cost to join:** Free

## Highs: What the site is good at and for ...

MySpace makes it easy for users to connect with potential customers and conduct viral marketing. Ample tools are available for customizing profile pages as well as sharing multimedia, such as videos or audio files. It's simple to search for and add friends, thereby expanding business networks. MySpace also features a classifieds section as well as group bulletins and one-on-one messaging.

### Lows: What's difficult or missing from the site …

MySpace offers users little in the way of customer service or support. The site has been dogged with security risks including excessive spam, "phishing" to fraudulently acquire sensitive information, and code issues that have allowed computer viruses to spread.

### Straight talk: If you're looking for these types of customers you should be on this site …

- MySpace is useful for businesses seeking teen and young adult customers.
- Those seeking pop-culture fans (American Idol or indie-rock bands, for example).
- Businesses targeting internet-savvy users.

### Another angle: This site could help grow your business if you're in one of the following categories …

- Businesses oriented toward teenagers, high-school and college students.
- Proprietors of online media sites such as photo or video sharing stand to benefit from joining the site, as will event promoters working in niches such as nightclub or concert venues or travel tours.

### A MySpace Profile Consists of …

Main picture: For a small business, this will typically be your logo rather than a personal picture. Make sure your logo is sufficiently clean and legible for the space allowed. If you're building a personal brand, use a nice or fun yet professional-looking photo of yourself.

URL: This will be myspace.com/yourbusiness. It's best if you're able to append your exact business name. For example, a business called ABC Enterprises would have the URL myspace.com/abcenterprises. If this isn't possible, keep as close as possible to the name of your business. Try adding your city—if ABC Enterprises were in Atlanta, the URL might be myspace.com/abcenterprisesatlanta.

**Message:** You can add a caption at the top of your profile page, next to the main picture or logo. This caption can say anything, be it clever, funny, descriptive, or inviting. Whatever your message, make it both powerful and memorable. You can change this message as often or seldom as you like.

**Personal information:** Make your profile fun even if you're promoting your business here, you can share likes, such as your affinity for Desperate Housewives and Radiohead. Make sure you provide full contact information for your business, as well as an overview of the services you're offering.

**My connections:** As with all social-networking sites, joining groups that either interest you or are related to your business provide opportunities to introduce yourself and network with thousands of potential fans who might not have found you on their own.

**About me:** Though some MySpace users have lengthy, elaborate bios, we recommend you don't follow their lead. Keep this section short and to the point. Explain exactly who you are, what you do, and why this should interest visitors to your profile page.

**Groups:** MySpace groups are organized under a range of categories including Business and Entrepreneurs, Computers and Internet, and Money and Investing. These are handy for connecting with others in your industry. It's also easy for users to search groups and find your profile page.

**Friends:** One of the most well-known features on MySpace, the Friends function allows users to find and connect with one another. As a small business, it's important for you to have MySpace friends in order to build your network. However, since these connections are visible to everyone visiting your profile page, you need to choose appropriate friends who actually understand your business and have made the choice to opt into your network. People who are your friends can leave comments, and it's considered polite to comment "Thanks for the add" when others add you as a friend. Keep track of your comments and remove those that are spam or not positive for your business. You can set controls to approve comments before they post live to your site page.

**Blog:** If your business doesn't already have a blog, MySpace provides an easy way to get one going. A useful tool to communicate with potential customers, a blog can also provide information, tips and tricks, and demonstrate your professional savvy in an accessible, easy-to-update format.

**Calendar:** If your business has special events, keep your calendar updated so customers can keep track of them.

### Site Add-ons

**Pictures:** You can upload numerous pictures that will only be available to registered, logged-in MySpace members. As a small business, you might want to display shots of product offerings, significant clients, or appropriate personal photos.

**Video:** There are several ways to upload video clips to your page. Many users simply embed videos that they've already posted to YouTube or other video-sharing sites. To do this, copy the embed code on your selected YouTube video and paste it to MySpace. You can post the video to your profile, to your blog, or in a comment. Keep videos on topic and relevant to the message you're trying to convey.

**Custom backgrounds and formatting:** MySpace offers nearly unlimited ways to customize your profile page. Once you've registered, you can use premade MySpace layouts, which come in literally hundreds of themes to suit your specific taste. MySpace graphics are also available. If you're comfortable with HTML coding, you can use it to customize colors, font sizes, styles, and other design details. We strongly recommend you keep your profile page as clean and easy to read as possible. Don't overload it with too many gadgets or you'll risk alienating potential clients.

### Site Customization Resources

Profile customization has become a cottage industry unto itself, with multiple sites competing to help you tweak your MySpace profile. Here are a few great resources to help you get started:

**Thomas' MySpace Editor:** strikefile.com/myspace. A popular, straightforward choice for customizing your page.

**MySpace Master:** myspacemaster.net. Profile customization tool offering layouts, codes, backgrounds, graphics, and generators.

**Profile Jewels:** bigoo.ws. A handy site for finding profile tools and add-ons.

**Tagtooga:** tagtooga.com/tapp/pages/ultimate.html. A self-proclaimed "ultimate MySpace customization code reference," this site helps you do everything from adding borders and tables to hiding potentially sensitive information.

**Lissa Explains It All**: A MySpace Tutorial: lissaexplains.com/myspace. The helpful Lissa tackles everything from contact tables to comments.

## Site Marketing and Advertising Opportunities

Social networking lets you promote your business in a number of creative ways. Here are a few ideas to get you started:

**Banner ads:** Try a targeted banner-ad campaign to publicize your services. These are a few companies that can help:

- **My Banner Maker:** mybannermaker.com. Banner creation for MySpace and other sites.
- **Pimp My Profile:** pimp-my-profile.com. Offers an online banner generator as well as customizable layouts.
- **MyBannerSpace:** mybannerspace.com. Extended network banner creation with a variety of themes
- **Style My Profile:** stylemyprofile.net/banner-maker. Custom banner and extended network banner creator that generates, then uploads banners, making it easy for users to cut and paste the embed code

**Classified ads:** It's free to post these ads on MySpace. They break down into 11 main categories, the most relevant of which to small businesses is the Services category. To post your ad, click on the Classifieds button on the top right part of the MySpace banner.

**Groups:** We recommend that you join at least three groups relevant to your business. As with classifieds, MySpace Groups break down into a series of main categories. The site currently has nearly 25,000 user-created groups dedicated to entrepreneurship and business. To get started, click the Groups button near the middle of the MySpace banner.

**Advertising widgets:** These rich media applications are simple to build, customize, and add to your profile page. One online resource for MySpace widgets is Widgetbox: widgetbox.com/tag/advertising. Widgetbox offers more than 1,000 advertising widgets including scrolling LED messages, online shopping resources, and real-time financial news and analysis.

**Books:** There's a host of print resources written by authors who want to help you expand your marketing and advertising activities on MySpace. Two such books are *Plug Your Business!* by Steve Weber: amazon.com/Business-Marketing-MySpace-podcasts-networks /dp/0977240622. Author Nick Jag has written *MySpace Marketing: The Promotional Revolution*, which can be found online here: nick-jag.com/marketing.

### Getting Started on MySpace

Follow these steps to launch your own MySpace profile and start expanding your business network:

On MySpace, click the Sign Up button at the top right corner. Fill in the required information. You'll then be prompted to upload a photo or logo, and to invite others to join. Fill in further information about your profile and begin customizing your page and searching for friends.

Remember that you won't be able to send messages, post comments, post bulletins, or add friends until you verify the e-mail address used to register.

# Hi5 (hi5.com)

## What Is It?

Offers a profile page, a friend request feature, photo storage, music reviews, a range of applications, video, and e-mail. Hi5 has a strong following of young Hispanic users, as well as users who are located in Central America. Hi5 is growing in popularity, especially in Spanish-speaking countries. According to Alexa.com, it ranks in the top 20 most visited sites. Its offerings follow suit with most of its competitors, yet friends are categorized by degree: first degree is direct friends, second degree is the friends of direct friends, and third degree is the friends of the friends of direct friends.

## Site Stats

**Born:** 2002
**Users:** About 99 million members
**Demographics:** Most users fall in the 13- to 24-year-old range
**Cost to join:** Free

### Highs: What the site is good at and for ...

With a vast member base, it's easy to network and promote your business through their basic offerings. It practically finds friends for you by suggesting the profiles of people you may know. Users can upload photos and videos on their profile. Videos can also be shared with all users, not just your friends.

### Lows: What's difficult or missing from the site ...

The site recently launched its hi5 platform, similar to Facebook, which includes applications for users. However, it wasn't very well received in its initial version. Music is only part of the site's applications and doesn't provide as strong an offering as other sites do. As with most social-network criticisms, it's easy to inadvertently find inappropriate profiles and postings. Only the first 100 applications (or widgets) made will be translated into Spanish from English; the majority of users are Spanish speakers.

**Straight talk: If you're looking for these types of customers you should be on this site ...**
- Teens and young adults
- Internet-savvy users
- Spanish speakers

**Another angle: This site could help grow your business if you're in one of the following categories...**
- Photo or video sharing online media
- Targeting teenagers or college students
- International business

## A Hi5 Profile Consists of ...

**Main picture:** For a small business, this will typically be your logo rather than a personal picture. Make sure your logo is sufficiently clean and legible for the space allowed.

**URL:** Choose your personal hi5 URL by clicking "My Profile" on the top of the page. Next to your profile picture, enter your business name in the info bar, and your link will be businessname.hi5.com. It's best to choose the name of your business or something close to it, so others can easily search and identify your page. If need be, you can use another identifier if your business name is already taken. For a San Francisco-based business, try businessnameSF.hi5.com.

**Status:** Your status lets people know your current mood or what you are up to, and is meant to be updated frequently. However, for a business profile, it may not be good to let hi5 members know you're bored. This would be a good place to mention news, promotions, a slogan, etc., that will appropriately reflect your business to the world. Your statuses are saved and can be viewed in your scrapbook.

**Personal info:** While it may not be imperative that your profile have a gender or birthday, it's important to provide valid contact information. Include an e-mail address, IM screename, phone number, address, and web address so potential customers can get in touch with you easily.

**About me:** In addition to a hometown and languages spoken, you can tell people all about your business. It's best to grab people with something interesting, short, and to the point.

**Groups:** There are several categories of groups on hi5, so it's likely that you can create your own group and join several others. This is a good way to find potential customers who are already interested in what your company offers. In these groups you can send messages and post related information.

**Friends:** Entering your e-mail address and password is one way to find friends on hi5. Sometimes the site can even find friends for you. On hi5 especially, an expansive friends list is important to growing your business because you become connected with friends of friends of friends. Keeping this in mind, some friends may not be worth having if they could potentially compromise the image of your company, so choose and accept them carefully. This may also mean you will have to monitor your profile for inappropriate comments.

**Blog:** Share what's going on with your company by posting blog updates. Even if you have a blog already, it may bring more people to your website if you have the information on hi5 with a link to the other post. Blogs can also help explain and demonstrate products, announce events, and give behind-the-scenes information. While these don't need to be updated every day, it's good to have about one post a week or so.

## Site Add-ons

**Pictures:** Small businesses would benefit from uploading photos related to products and services. However, posting photos of significant clients, events, a creative officer, or other extras could make your company friendlier and your profile more like a fan page.

**Videos:** Videos allow potential customers to learn more about your company's offerings in a fun and memorable way. You can even set up a channel where people can subscribe to make sure they don't miss the latest videos. Uploaded videos can be seen by any hi5 member. Music is currently only offered by a handful of applications. To download your choice of players, click "Find Music" under the My Profile page.

**Skins:** There are many skins to choose from on the site. You can also customize your site's design; however, it would take a basic knowledge of HTML. It would be wise to use your company's logo or signature style and colors in your design for a streamlined branding approach. And as always, keep it simple and to the point.

Site customization resources: Jazz up your profile with a custom skin. While it requires basic HTML skills, it will help set your page apart from the masses.

**Skin Customizer:** hi5.com/friend/account/displayEditProfileSkin.do. As profile design is based on "skins," hi5 has a form to create a custom skin.

## Site Marketing and Advertising Opportunities

**Banner ads:** While banner ads are placed at the bottom of profiles, they can still be an effective means of advertising. These are a few companies that can help:

- **My Banner Maker:** mybannermaker.com. Banner creation for hi5 and other sites
- **Pimp My Profile:** pimp-my-profile.com. Offers an online banner generator as well as customizable layouts
- **MyBannerSpace:** mybannerspace.com. Extended network banner creation with a variety of themes
- **Style My Profile:** stylemyprofile.net/banner-maker. Custom banner and extended network banner creator that generates, then uploads banners, making it easy for users to cut and paste the embed code

**Groups:** Getting involved in several groups is a great way to reach a target audience. Communicate promotions, events, and new products via messaging and forum postings. Currently, the site has about 1.5 million groups.

**hi5 platform:** Groups can create their own applications to be a part of the hi5 community. Some companies create applications to show off their business or even games that can be used to promote the services in a fun way. Since each site is different in its requirements, it's best to inquire about these directly: hi5networks.com/developer.

## Getting Started on hi5

Follow these steps to launch your own hi5 profile and start expanding your business network:

- On hi5, fill out the information in the yellow box that says "Sign Up for hi5." You'll be required to enter your e-mail address password to see if your e-mail contacts may already be hi5 members.
- On your profile page, you can edit everything from a photo to your "status" at the moment.
- After you've filled in your information, it's time to start searching for friends. Remember that you won't be able to interact with others until you add them as friends.

## Insider Tips

- Because the majority of users are in Spanish-speaking countries, you may want to explore translation options and take cultural practices into consideration.
- Even though the open platform hasn't performed well, if you decide to stick with the site, stick with the applications and widgets. These are the latest advertising trend that users are actually enjoying. So make yours something they can't resist.
- Definitely customize a skin to represent your business. Users visit many profiles each day, so they need to associate your business with strong branding.

---

# Bebo (bebo.com)

## What Is It?

A hybrid of MySpace and Facebook, Bebo targets college students. Their motto is "Blog Early, Blog Often." The site has more than 40 million members and is the largest social networking site in the UK, Ireland, and New Zealand. In the U.S. Bebo ranks third behind

MySpace and Facebook. In 2006, it was the People's Vote for the Webby Award the best social networking site. In March 2008, the site was acquired by AOL for $850 million.

## Site Stats
**Born:** July 2005
**Users:** 40 million
**Demographics:** Most users are 16–22 years old
**Cost to join:** Free

### Highs: What the site is good at and for ...
Easy for users to connect with potential customers and conduct viral marketing. While some social networking sites have run into criticisms over safety, the site allows profiles to be private to anyone but friends. Businesses can create applications and widgets, which are widely used among members. Profiles have several methods for interacting with other members, meaning there's a lot of time spent looking at profiles.

### Lows: What's difficult or missing from the site ...
The strides for safety could hinder connectivity with potential clients. Being internationally popular may make it difficult for businesses solely based in the U.S. It has yet to surpass Facebook or MySpace, meaning people may not feel the need to sign up for another site that offers similar features in its early U.S. stages. Usernames are not unique, as they are based on members' first and last names, making profile identification and URLs difficult to predict.

### Straight Talk: If you're looking for these types of customers you should be on this site ...
- Teens and young adults
- Internet-savvy users
- Pop-culture fans (American Idol watchers or indie-rock bands, etc.)

### Another angle: This site could help grow your business if you're in one of the following categories ...
- Photo or video sharing online media
- Targeting teenagers or college students

- Event promotion (concerts, nightclubs, travel tours, etc.)
- International and/or web-based

## Bebo Profiles Consist of ...

**Main picture:** Make it easy for users to identify you by uploading a logo. Make sure your logo is sufficiently clean and legible for the space allowed.

**URL:** Since Bebo profiles are private by default, you'll have to click "Get your URL" link next to your main picture. As usernames go by first and last names, it's difficult to know what the automated URL will be. You may find it helpful to search for your business' name on the site before you create a profile.

**Message:** It's literally a speech bubble coming from your main picture. It may be a good place to stick your company logo, or even something funny, clever, or welcoming. And it can be changed as often as you like. Keep in mind, as with everything on your profile, it's meant to represent your business.

**Personal info:** Called "Me, My Life and I," it's a space to tell everyone about your business. While you could list your must-TiVo TV, it's better to be simple and direct about your company and what it offers. So be sure to include full contact information and a general overview.

**Groups:** Bebo groups aren't categorized, but instead are accessed by rank, featured groups, and friends' groups. They are an easy way to find like-minded people. Promoting your business in this area is as simple as creating your own group and sending information to members through messages.

**Friends:** Typical of most social networking sites, Bebo allows you to connect with others through friends. To grow your business, it's important to have a lot of friends to widen your network. Since friends are visible on your profile, make sure they're also reflecting the image you want your business to portray. Friends can leave comments on your profile, so monitoring this is key to remove inappropriate postings and to respond to maintain relationships with contacts.

**Blog:** To keep your contacts updated on everything your business is doing, make sure to share it on your Bebo blog. Adding tips and tricks, extra information, and behind-the-scenes action will enhance the overall experience of your customers.

**Extras and applications:** The bulk of the profile consists of applications and extras, such as photos and videos. With so many options, it's easy to go overboard with these and the result will be a crowded and confusing profile. Keep it simple.

## Site Add-ons

**Pictures:** Uploaded photos are sorted by albums and are visible to all Bebo users. Use this feature to put a face to your business. Photos can be of products, events, or even appropriate personal photos.

**Videos:** Videos are a dynamic way to share your company's products, mission, etc. There are several ways to upload video clips to your page. Videos can be uploaded directly from your computer or by embedding links from video-sharing sites like YouTube.

**Music:** Bebo Music is a part of the Groups section. Your favorite bands can be added to your profile, but only take advantage if it's appropriate for your business. You don't want any features to distract from other, more essential elements of your profile.

**Skins:** Bebo has thousands of skins (or designs) to search through and use to set your profile apart. We strongly recommend that you keep your profile page as clean and easy to read as possible. Don't overload it with too many gadgets or you'll risk alienating potential clients. See below on how to create a custom skin.

### Skin Customization Resources

Profile skin customization has become a cottage industry unto itself, with multiple sites competing to help you tweak your Bebo profile. Create your own at bebo.com/. The site has its own tutorial on how to create a customized skin. It may take some design software know-how, but it would be beneficial for your skin to be consistent with your business branding.

### Site Marketing and Advertising Opportunities

Social networking lets you promote your business in a number of creative ways. Here are a few ideas to get you started:

**Bebo Nation:** You can stake a visual claim in Bebo Nation, a virtual, graphical country. A 10 by 10 pixel space, perfect for a photo or logo, runs for 10 cents and is never deleted. The images can link to a profile, group, or band profile. Availability is determined by remaining land.

**Groups:** Joining several groups can gain you direct access to potential customers. With so many categories, it's easy to get the word out to interested users or create your own. To get started, click "Explore" and then "Groups."

**Advertising widgets:** A popular way to provide an interactive advertising experience is through widgets/applications. One online resource for Bebo widgets is Widgetbox: widgetbox.com/tag/advertising. Widgetbox offers more than 1,000 advertising widgets, including scrolling LED messages, online shopping resources, and real-time financial news and analysis.

**Books:** Several books can help you navigate the online waters of social-networking for your business. Be sure to check out *Marketing to the Social Web* by Larry Weber and Steve Weber's *Plug Your Business!*

### Getting Started on Bebo

Follow these steps to launch your own Bebo profile and start expanding your business network:

- On Bebo.com, click the Sign Up button at the top right corner.
- Fill in the required information. You'll be prompted to enter your e-mail address and password to find e-mail contacts that may already be on Bebo.
- From here you'll be able to fill in further information about your profile, upload a photo, and customize your page, and search for friends. Remember that you won't be able to send

messages, post comments, post bulletins, or add friends until you verify the e-mail address used to register.

### Insider Tips

- Users enjoy using fun widgets/applications. Incorporate one for your business.
- Whatever your design or text, keep it professional. You want to build friendships and be fun, but you're a member because you want to grow your business. If you want to share personal information, consider having two accounts.

---

# Friendster (friendster.com)

### What Is It?

Credited as one of the first online social networks, Friendster helps users stay in touch with friends and discover new people and interests important to them. Friendster targets an adult audience of 18 years and up and is currently most used in Asia. It's no longer a major player in the U.S. Friendster is a pure social-networking site that's heavy on its social aspects (to the point of bordering on a dating site) and fairly light on the networking. The site includes typical information such as name, age, location, and the types of people whom users are interested in meeting. An internal search engine powered by Google allows users to search for existing friends or find new ones. You can also join groups, start groups, participate in forums, or create a blog. However, the main reason to be on Friendster seems to lie in its association with Google and the power of creating a fan profile, which separates friends from fans in order to give select businesses and entities the ability to more efficiently market themselves throughout the site.

### Site Stats

**Born:** March 2002.
**Users:** More 50 million, a majority of which are in Asia.
**Demographics:** Urban, liberal, tech-savvy, 24–35 age range
**Cost to join:** Free

**Highs: What the site is good at and for ...**

The site is easy to navigate, with a permanent menu toolbar at the top of each page, extra links on individual pages, and links on profile pages. Friendster's search function is also simple to use when looking for other site members by keyword or other criteria. Friendster's Groups function lets members choose communities from more than 30 major categories, allowing entrepreneurs to tap into existing networks of potential customers. The site's networking features let users customize their profile pages, upload photos, graphics, videos, and music, and see the last 100 people who viewed their profile.

**Lows: What's difficult or missing from the site ...**

Though Friendster asks members to report offensive content, the site has received criticism for failure to remove such content in a timely manner. The site has lost favor with many users over time and is not the social networking powerhouse it once was.

**Straight talk: If you're looking for these types of customers you should be on this site ...**

- Tech-savvy users in the 24–35 age range
- Users in Asia
- Older, tech-savvy internet users the 35-and-up crowd

**Another angle: This site could help grow your business if you're in one of the following categories ...**

- Photo or video sharing online media sites
- Businesses targeting an Asian clientele
- Online dating media sites

## A Friendster Profile Consists of ...

**Fan profile:** To give select businesses and entities the ability to market more effectively throughout the site, Friendster separates friends from fans. Fan profiles are meant to provide a sustainable cycle of marketing that can happen virally without much input from you. This is the best kind of marketing! After you've created a profile, you can apply to have it converted to a fan profile. These allow entrepreneurs to more easily tap into Friendster's 50-plus million members. As your fan base grows, you can connect to an unlimited number of your fans through Friendster's robust mail system.

Perhaps the greatest benefit is that Friendster profiles are searchable through Google, Yahoo!, MSN, and other search engines, so as your profile gains fans, your information gets indexed higher in search results. Your page comes with "key tags" used by all major search engines when indexing content, and the strength of these search terms will also help determine how easy it is to find you on Friendster and through the search engines. Make sure to optimize your page with key tags, which in turn will help you rise in the search rankings, drive more traffic to your profile, and add fans, again increasing your ranking in the search engines.

When your Fan Profile launches, Friendster will help promote you through its "new discovery modules." You'll be featured on the Friendster website and in the global newsletter. Though valuable, these promotions are brief, so make sure your content is complete and accurate before upgrading to the Fan Profile.

Fan Profiles also let you automatically send an e-mail whenever you update your blog or post new content. You can further reduce maintenance by setting your site to automatically accept fan requests. Once a member clicks the "Become A Fan" button, he or she will be added to your network.

**Classifieds:** The best advertising is free advertising. Friendster's classifieds section fits the bill and is available from the homepage and every other page after that. Just look to the top right

**My Apps:** Friendster's suite of third-party applications can help you expand from the basic content of your profile and blog. Though many of these applications don't have direct business uses, using them creatively can help give potential customers an in-depth look at who you are and what makes your products and services unique. Choose from more than 250 applications (for a total of 12 applications per profile). The list is continually changing, but here are a few ways that applications can help pump your Friendster profile:

- Add playlists, songs, photos, and videos

- Create avatars and play interactive games (your avatar actually cheers you on)
- Build custom slideshows and skins
- Join chat rooms with text, audio, and video
- Sync your iTunes library directly with your Friendster profile
- Import YouTube videos and create custom players
- Show your support for good causes worldwide
- Interact with your fans by letting them post comments, photos, and even videos directly on your profile

**My Connections:** As with all social-networking sites, joining groups that either interest you or are related to your business provide opportunities to introduce yourself and network with thousands of potential fans who might not have found you on their own.

**Explore:** Forums offer the opportunity to become an expert in your field by answering questions in areas where you may have valuable information. However, if you're seeking answers to your own questions, a better destination may be LinkedIn, unless you're looking to learn more about Friendster itself. In that event, you'll find a variety of experts who can help guide you through the technical aspects of improving your profile and blog. Just don't be surprised if those experts are 18!

**Search:** Friendster's search function is powered by Google, which is the site's exclusive provider of both search and keyword-targeted advertising. You can either search within the site or throughout the internet, with results powered by what is arguably the number-one search engine around.

**Invite:** The Invite feature allows you to provide the e-mail addresses of friends you'd like to invite to use Friendster. Once those friends accept the invitation, they are automatically added to your network.

## Site Add-ons
**Music:** Add music to your Friendster profile. Here's one resource that can help get you started: toxxic.net/music1.php.

**Flash Links and Sidebar Navigation:** To add either flash links or sidebar navigation to your Friendster profile, visit flashvortex.com. From there:

- Choose your desired buttons and designs.
- Input your button labels and links.
- Select your layout option.
- Generate your codes and click Download. From here, you can insert your code into your profile.

**Guestbook:** Add a free guestbook to your profile by visiting 123guestbook.com. This could be particularly useful for small businesses looking to collect contact information from potential customers who have visited your profile.

**Videos:** To add video to your Friendster profile, visit friendster.com/video.php#src = youtube&id = nssrqK-0VUg. From here you can choose from a whole host of video offerings. Make sure your video selection is appropriate to your business and its products and services.

## Site Customization Resources

There are multiple resources available to help you tweak your Friendster profile. Here are a few to get you started:

**Hot Friendster Layouts:** hotfriendsterlayouts.com/TestimonialGraphics.htm. A one-stop shop for premade Friendster layouts, free of charge.

**Friendster Tweakers:** friendster-tweakers.com/. More Friendster layout customization tools, including a profile editor, codes, glitter, and graphic icons.

**Profile Jewels:** bigoo.ws. A handy site for finding profile tools and add-ons, including those for Friendster.

**Friendster Code:** friendstercode.net. Codes to help tweak your Friendster profile.

**My Custom Profile:** mycustomprofile.com. Offers custom layouts for many social networking sites, including Friendster.

## Site Marketing and Advertising Opportunities

Social networking lets you promote your business in a number of creative ways. Here are a few ideas to get you started:

**Fan Profiles:** Fan Profiles are one of the most powerful ways of marketing on Friendster. These are designed to create sustainable marketing cycles that don't require much input from you. By optimizing your Fan Profile with key tags, you'll rise in search engine rankings and drive more traffic to your profile, which in turn will drive fans. With each fan you add, you'll continue to get even more exposure.

**Blogs:** Friendster Blogs are a powerful way to get the message out about your business and to show your professional knowledge. Keep these professional, relevant, on-topic, and informative and you'll see potential customers coming back.

**Groups:** As with groups on other social networking sites, Friendster Groups allow entrepreneurs to tap into active communities of potential customers. The site has more than 30 main categories of groups from which to choose.

**Paid Advertising:** Paid advertising is also available on Friendster. For more information, contact the site directly at adsales@friendster.com.

## Getting Started on Friendster

Follow these steps to launch your own Friendster profile and start expanding your business network:

- On Friendster, click the red Sign Up button to the right.
- Fill in the required information.

From here you can fill in further information about your profile and begin customizing your page and searching for friends. Remember that you won't be able to send messages, post comments, post bulletins, or add friends until you verify the e-mail address used to register.

# Xanga (xanga.com)

## What Is It?

A community where users can start a free weblog, share photos and videos, and meet new friends. With a mostly teen audience, Xanga sites are most commonly used as personal journals. Xanga—pronounced ZANG-uh—acts as a virtual journal for its members to share with the world. It has expanded to offer different forms of journaling, including blogs, photo blogs, video blogs (or vlogs), and audio blogs. Based in New York City, the site has expanded its offerings since debuting in 2000, but has not been gaining many new users lately.

## Site Stats

**Born:** 2000

**Users:** 27 million bloggers as of August 2006

**Demographics:** About 20 percent are ages 12–17 and 35 percent are ages 35–54; most users are from Hong Kong and the United States

**Cost to join:** Free, but Xanga Premium runs at $25 for a year or $100 for a lifetime, while Premium Plus costs $45 per year

### Highs: What the site is good at and for ...

It's easy to update people on company news in a variety of mediums. Blogrings are like groups, in that people join together under common interests. Xanga Footprints shows users which subscribers are looking at their profiles. Users can also choose to opt out of this feature. Non-registered members are tracked by country. Comments on each type of blog encourage community and open dialog.

### Lows: What's difficult or missing from the site ...

Nielsen Net Ratings shows that Xanga was down 44 percent in popularity from August 2006 to August 2007, while Facebook was up 117 percent and MySpace was up 23 percent in the same time frame. Some members have joined and created blogs solely to "cyber bully" others. There have been several incidents leading to law enforcement intervention as blogs were used to make threats and post inappropriate content. Critics say the design of profiles and the site isn't up to par with its competitors and even customized pages still lack design freedom.

**Straight talk: If you're looking for these types of customers you should be on this site ...**
- Teens and young adults
- Internet-savvy users
- Photo and video users

**Another angle: This site could help grow your business if you're in one of the following categories ...**
- Photo or video sharing
- Targeting teenagers or college students
- Have frequent updates

## Xanga Profiles Consist of ...

**Main picture:** In representing your company, consider uploading a logo for your main profile photo. Make sure it's clean and easy to read in the space provided.

**URL:** Your username will be attached to your profile and your web link. It's wise to choose a name as close to your company name as possible, because the URL will look like xanga.com/businessname. This is especially important in terms of people searching for you. If your name is already taken, consider other ways to easily identify your business. If your company is located in New York City, your username could be BusinessNameNYC.

**Personal info:** Avoid telling people your favorite sports teams and what celebrity fan club you're in; this is where you tell people about your business. Include contact information, your region (if applicable), and a brief statement about your company.

**Friends:** When you first sign up, you'll have three friends to teach you more about the site: The XangaTeam, Featured Questions, and Featured Weblogs. Having more friends is the best way to build up your network. Friends can comment and interact on your profile and blogs, so it's important to keep in mind that they're also a reflection of your company. Monitor their activity and ban the ones who don't seem to be a good fit. It's also a good idea to reciprocate the positive activity that comes from your new friends.

**Blog:** This is the main part of the site; it'll be the primary focus of your profile. Be sure to keep it updated with new information to keep users coming back for more. You can blog about company news, how-tos, new products, public events, and more.

**Pulse:** If you only have a quick moment to blog a little note, Pulse is the place to do it. While it doesn't show up on the main page, your updates are displayed in real time on the Pulse homepage. These tidbits are saved and can also serve as a milestone timeline.

## Site Add-ons

**Pictures:** Don't just tell people what you're about—show them with photos. You can upload photos into albums and include caption information to get your point across. You may also want to include bonus photos that show what your company is like. Whether it's day-to-day or a special event, photos grab people more than text. Keep this in mind when you're choosing images.

**Videos:** Videos are another way to provide an in-depth look at your business. You can upload videos directly through the site and they'll be accessible to any users through a link on your profile.

**Premium and Premium Plus:** Xanga Premium is an upgraded account that runs $4 for 1 month, $15 for 6 months, $25 for a year, or $100 for a lifetime. It includes 10 GB of image hosting, more profile pictures, ad-free designs, a subscription browser, downloadable archives, and exclusive Xanga skins. Premium Plus offers similar features, but has many unlimited features. It costs $7 for 1 month, $24 for 6 months, or $45 for a year.

**Custom backgrounds and skins:** Backgrounds and skins are just one way to spice up your Xanga profile. Continue branding your business through skins and backgrounds (although some may be limited to premium accounts). Xanga has some of these to choose from or you can create your own with specific colors, fonts, and images by using tools on other websites. This may require some basic HTML knowledge. Keep it simple so as not to dilute your brand.

## Site Customization Resources

Profile customization has become a cottage industry unto itself, with multiple sites competing to help you tweak your Xanga profile. Here are a few resources to help you get started:

**Create Blog:** createblog.com. This site offers many creative options for many social networking sites.

**Doobix:** doobix.com/generators/xanga. A profile generator to provide a custom look for your page.

**Profile.jewels:** bigoo.ws. A handy site for finding profile tools and add-ons.

**Web Monkey:** webmonkey.com. HTML cheat-sheet and color help.

## Site Marketing and Advertising Opportunities

Social networking lets you promote your business in a number of creative ways. Here are a few ideas to get you started:

**Banner ads:** Try a targeted banner-ad campaign to publicize your services. These are a few companies that can help:
- **My Banner Maker:** mybannermaker.com. Banner creation for many sites.
- **Pimp My Profile:** pimp-my-profile.com. Offers an online banner generator as well as customizable layouts.
- **Style My Profile:** stylemyprofile.net/banner-maker. Custom banner and extended network banner creator that generates, then uploads banners, making it easy for users to cut and paste the embed code.

**Blogrings:** Like groups, Blogrings combine people of similar interests. Broken into categories such as Arts and Humanities, Games, and Society & Culture, blogrings can help a business target and communicate with potential customers easily. As an active member, your profile will also likely be of interest to other blogring members.

### Getting Started on Xanga

It's easy to join Xanga; follow these steps to sign up your business:

- On Xanga, click the green box that says "Join Xanga Now!"
- From there you'll fill out the required information, and start to fill out your profile information and upload a photo.

With your profile completed, it's time to search for friends, join blogrings, and start blogging.

### Insider Tips

- Video equipment and training are great investments if you're looking to maintain a vlog on Xanga.
- Update frequently! It's not a matter of putting together a great piece of literature, but rather giving the people what they want. Consider planning ahead on themes and ideas to save time and energy.
- Even if your website includes a blog and/or news feed, duplicate it on Xanga. You'll have a wider audience as a part of the network.

---

## Twitter (twitter.com)

### What Is It?

A social networking and microblogging service using instant messaging, SMS, or a web interface, Twitter asks users: "What are you doing?" The answer for small businesses: advertising in 140-character fragments to a hyperactive online audience. The site is operated by San Francisco–based Obvious, LLC and won the 2007 South by Southwest Web Award in the blog category. It's considered to be the next step in blogging, or microblogging, which focuses on rapid and frequent postings of brief musings.

### Site Stats

**Born:** October 2006

**Users:** While the company doesn't give out demographic information, TwitDir.com, a fan site that serves as a directory of Twitter users, reported 3,000,000 total Twitter accounts, with an average of

2,000 users joining each day as of July 2007. It has become much more popular since these stats were issued.

**Demographics:** Although not confirmed by the site, most users are considered to be early adopters in the tech industry and teens to 20-somethings who are comfortable navigating social networking sites and mobile devices.

**Cost to join:** Free

### Highs: What the site is good at and for ...

Connecting busy people and allowing others to share in their thoughts and experiences. Collaborating with other new media, such as instant messaging, texting, and third-party websites Facebook and Twitterrific. Searching users by region could benefit brick-and-mortar businesses. Creating a new type of blogging/online self-expression in a news feed format that even non-users can follow. CNN and other well-known organizations are using Twitter as a news feed.

### Lows: What's difficult or missing from the site ...

Banner-type advertising isn't currently available. Commercial posting is allowed, but complaints of spamming could lead to a blocked profile and/or general distrust of commercial users. Searching for specific users (individuals or businesses) can be difficult, as identity is based on a username. Concept is vague and it takes three links to explain the site's purpose to prospective users. Posts are meant to be frequent and brief, which could be difficult for companies who don't have new information to report throughout the day. Critics see typical users' posts to be superfluous and say the idea could be an invasion of privacy. Followers are listed by picture, not name, which could make it harder for businesses to stand out on users' profiles without strong branding.

### Straight talk: If you're looking for these types of customers you should be on this site ...

- Internet- and mobile device–savvy users
- People looking to connect via new technology
- Busy people

**Another angle: This site could help grow your business if you're in one of the following categories ,,,**
- Targeting teenagers or college students
- Developing mobile or internet programs to work with the site
- Having frequent information to share with followers

## Twitter Profiles Consist of ...

**Picture profile and user name:** A small user picture and username serve as the header of the page in the site's signature minimalist style. Use a logo and business name to improve search indexing.

**URL:** The link directing people to your business will look something like this: twitter.com/businessname. For people to find it easily, keep it simple and as close to your business name as possible. For example, a business called ABC Enterprises would have the URL twitter.com/abcenterprises. If the name is taken, keep as close as possible to the name of your business. Try adding your city: If ABC Enterprises were in Atlanta, the URL might be twitter.com/abcente prisesatlanta.

**Updates:** Brief text updates (or "tweets") answer the site's driving question—"What are you doing?" Small businesses could use this feature by frequently sharing company updates, advances, or promotions. Each post is limited to 140 characters—which includes letters, spaces, and punctuation. Posts include a timestamp and the method used for posting (e.g., via text messaging, IM, or online). The most recent update is in a larger font atop the previous updates. At the bottom of the page, a link to an RSS feed allows users or non-users to subscribe to updates.

**About:** Describe your business by name, location, website, and a bio statement on the top of the sidebar. As with the site's other features, the descriptions are meant to be short.

**Stats:** These are statistics specific to your profile: how many people you're following, how many people are following you, your favorite users, and the number of total updates you've written. The more followers (or subscribers) you have, the better.

**Following:** This is a list with tiny thumbnail profile pictures of subscribers that you chose to follow. You can follow people you're interested in or specific to hobbies, business, industry, mentors, etc. The following is automatically generated in your sidebar.

**Followers:** This is a list of people who choose to follow you. Your focus should on building your followers. Followers are the ones who see your tweets/posts and they can choose to forward them to their network of followers, which can expand your reach into the millions.

## Site Add-ons

Custom backgrounds and formatting: You can change the default design of a profile by uploading a background image or playing with the colors of the boxes and text that make up your profile. This may be easier for someone with a basic knowledge of HTML, but can be learned quickly. By customizing your page, it would set you apart from other users and be another way to reflect your brand. Options to customize are fairly limited.

## Site Marketing and Advertising Opportunities

Currently, Twitter doesn't offer advertising in the form of banner ads, widgets, groups, etc.; however, the company is developing advertising opportunities. Companies must formulate a more creative approach to reach users through creating a profile. Commercial users are allowed, but could be blocked by the site if other users complain of spam or other potential abuses of the site.

## Getting Started on Twitter

Follow these steps to launch your own Twitter profile and start expanding your business network:

- On Twitter, click the green "Get Started—Join!" button in the center of the page.
- Fill in the required information: username, password, and word verification.
- Next, fill in your e-mail address and e-mail password so the site can automatically find e-mail contacts that have Twitter accounts. The privacy policy assures this information is not stored.

Once in the home section, write an update using up to 140 characters. Posts usually answer, "What are you doing?" They can also update followers about a promotion or company news. To edit your account and profile, click "Settings" at the top of the page and fill out the desired information. To find users, search by name or location in the search bar at the top of the page. Or invite friends via e-mail.

## Insider Tips

- Twitter is all about minimalism—frequent minimalism. Keep that in mind when you're using the site to promote your business.
- While the site may thrive on spontaneity, it may be in your company's best interest to have a general plan for these postings.
- To organize your posts, consider coming up with a short phrase as a preface. For example: NEWS: Today we joined with Company Y and Z and have become Company XYZ; BACKSTAGE PASS: Ted just brought cake to the office to celebrate our first year of business!

## Social Networking Lingo for Twitter

Aside from the glossary of terms in this book, it is important that you understand what your social reach, velocity, and capital mean on Twitter, and what they can do for your business. A site called Twinfluence offers the best explanation of these terms. I have included a few of their tips below along with my own personal experience with my social networking on Twitter as well as clients.

Your *social reach* is the number of followers a Twitterer has or what is called "first-order followers. The second order of followers would be all of your followers plus their followers." Social reach is a measurement of potential audience and listeners, a best estimate of the number of people that a given Twitterer could quickly get a message to.

Your *social velocity* averages the number of first- and second-order followers attracted per day since the Twitterer first established his or her account. The larger the number is, the faster that

Twitterer has accumulated their influence. This number can jump significantly with the addition of a few high-profile followers. Velocity is scored from "very slow" to "very fast" relative to other twitterers at your network size. As twitterers build their follower network, their velocity tends to increase. The more followers you get and the faster you get them, then the faster your reach builds a "snowball" effect!

*Social capital* is a measure of how influential a Twitterer's followers are. A high value indicates that most of that Twitterer's followers have a lot of followers themselves. Social capital is scored from "very low" to "very high" relative to other Twitterers at your network size.

---

# Tagged (tagged.com)

## What Is It?

Touted as the fastest-growing social networking site, Tagged seeks to reach the youth market by offering profile pages, quizzes, journals, instant messaging, chat rooms, and more. The site is based in San Francisco and received $7 million in funding from the Mayfield Fund in early 2006.

## Site Stats

**Born:** October 2004

**Users:** 30 million registered members, with 10 million unique visitors each month

**Demographics:** 63 percent are 18 and older, with 60 percent female and 40 percent male

**Cost to join:** Free

### Highs: What the site is good at and for ...

There are several ways for users to connect, leading to vast networking possibilities. Profile designs are customizable and they don't take HTML knowledge to figure out. Finding friends is easy, as you can search by age, location, gender, and more. Widgets are popular among users and enhance profiles. They also provide a slick new advertising opportunity.

### Lows: What's difficult or missing from the site ...

Inappropriate content is far too easy to find. The site has been criticized for sketchy tactics in getting new members to get friends to join. After collecting a new member's e-mail address and password, Tagged scours contacts and e-mails everyone to join the site as if it were the new member. This has led many people to consider it a "spam site."

### Straight talk: If you're looking for these types of customers you should be on this site ...

- Teens and young adults
- Internet-savvy users
- Those looking for dating, relationships
- Online game players

### Another angle: This site could help grow your business if you're in one of the following categories ...

- Photo or video sharing online
- Targeting teenagers or college students
- Online game developers

### Tagged Profiles Consist of ...

**Main picture:** Consider choosing your company's logo for a profile picture, to make it easily identifiable.

**URL:** Your Tagged URL isn't based on the name you enter when you sign up. To select a URL, go to your profile and click to select a URL. Enter your business name to check availability. If all goes well, your URL will be tagged.com/businessname. Only letters, numbers, and underscores are permitted in the name.

**About me:** While gender, age, and location are automatically displayed, you can write more personal information to share with other users. Keep this a clear and concise description of your business and why visitors should be interested in you. Don't forget to include contact information so they can easily find your services.

**Friends:** Keeping a large network of friends is a sure way to expand your company's horizons. Friends can interact with you on your profile and content, but this interaction should be monitored. Some friends are not worth having if they post inappropriate content that could jeopardize the image of your company. For those who prove themselves to be good friends, it's polite to show some support in return.

**Blog:** Called a journal on Tagged, it is an easy way to share your company's updates. Simply type up a paragraph or two about a new product, upcoming event, etc., so your subscribers will feel plugged in. These are meant to be updated fairly frequently, so don't let too much time pass in between posts.

**Luv:** Show your friends some "luv" by upping their LuvMeter. It's a silly way to show a friend some appreciation, and who knows, someone might luv you back!

## Site Add-ons

**Pictures:** Fill a photo gallery with pictures of new products, recent events, how-tos, or even office life. A visual display can enhance users' understanding of your business and be more attractive than text.

**Videos:** Videos are another great way to show what your company does. You can upload videos on the site or embed videos from YouTube or other sites in comments and other text boxes where HTML code is permitted. As with everything that appears on your profile—keep it relevant to your company's mission and image.

**Widgets:** A variety of widgets is available for your profile. Categories range from photos to voice, music to toys. While it may be fun to have one or two of these, it's best to keep your profile simple.

**Custom backgrounds and formatting:** Choosing a style is simple on Tagged, as there are many templates to choose from. You can also customize your profile's colors, background image, fonts, and font colors by clicking "Create a New Style" on the Style page. The best part about this is that it doesn't take any HTML knowledge and is shown in a preview so there isn't as much guesswork. This is a great opportunity to reinforce your company's brand.

## Site Customization Resources

While Tagged offers custom layouts, you may want to try out what many others have come up with in these online resources:

**Imhaven:** imhaven.com/tagged-layouts.htm. There are many themes for background styles.

**Profile.jewels:** bigoo.ws. A handy site for finding profile tools and add-ons.

## Site Marketing and Advertising Opportunities

Social networking lets you promote your business in a number of creative ways. Here are a few ideas to get you started:

**Banner ads:** There are several sizes of banner ads available on Tagged, as well as skins, rich media, and e-mail newsletters. These are a few companies that can help:

- **My Banner Maker:** mybannermaker.com. Banner creation for many sites
- **Pimp My Profile:** pimp-my-profile.com. Offers an online banner generator as well as customizable layouts
- **MyBannerSpace:** mybannerspace.com. Extended network banner creation with a variety of themes
- **Style My Profile:** stylemyprofile.net/banner-maker. Custom banner and extended network banner creator that generates, then uploads banners, making it easy for users to cut and paste the embed code

**Contests and games:** Brand integration can be done through sponsored profiles, homepage takeovers, and various contests and promotions. Users can interact with this kind of advertising and prefer a fun game over blatant advertisement.

**Advertising widgets:** The latest in social networking fun is the use of widgets. They allow users to customize their profile, play games, and interact with others through these rich media applications.

Widget box (widgetbox.com/tag/advertising) offers more than 1,000 advertising widgets, including scrolling LED messages, online shopping resources, and real-time financial news and analysis.

## Getting Started on Tagged

Using this guide, you can join Tagged, build your profile, and connect with thousands if not millions of potential customers:

- On Tagged, click the orange "Join Free!" button and enter the required information.
- Fill out your profile, add some pictures, and search for friends to build your network.
- Continue to customize your profile with a template or custom style.
- Write a journal post, search for widgets and you're on your way.

## Insider Tips

Having fun is the core of this social networking site. Get your business in on the action through an application/widget. Usually a game or another interactive way to connect with friends, these are a great way to get people excited about your offerings. However, it's important to think outside the box for these, due to heavy competition.

Make use of the blog! People want to feel a part of the action, so keep them updated on new products and offerings, as well as what's going on behind the scenes. Social networking marketing is all about connections—make them quality ones.

---

# BlitzTime (BlitzTime.com)

## What Is It?

Although this is a newer site to the networking front, they are moving up the presence ladder. This up-and-coming site offers networking events from your telephone. The site offers Blitz sessions and events that you can join based on your area of interest. You can hear each member in the session give a brief talk about themselves and what they have to offer, you can then choose to add them to your Blitz network and further the conversation or pass onto the next person. Blitz is based in a suburb of Boston.

## Site Stats

**Born:** October 2007.

**Users:** As of March 31, 2009 there were over 3,000 people registered on BlitzTime, over 1,000 of whom had attended a BlitzTime event.

**Demographics:** Specific demographics were not available at the time of our research as this is a newer site; their target market is active networkers that attend networking events to grow their business or enrich themselves.

**Cost to join:** There is no cost to sign up initially; when you register you get 2 free event credits that you can use at most BlitzTime events. If you want to continue blitzing (attending BlitzTime events) after you've used your 2 free credits you must become a Professional Subscriber. The price for the Professional Subscription is $19.95/month and that gives you the ability to attend virtually all BlitzTime events (you may be restricted from private events and you may need to pay more for select events, with the price decided by the event host). When you become a Professional Subscriber you also get the ability to host events.

### Highs: What the site is good at and for ...

It's nice to be able to chat with potential clients, customers, or partners voice to voice and quickly. It's fairly easy to set up your profile. You can post an audio introduction on your profile for others to listen to. You can host or attend events.

### Lows: What's difficult or missing from the site ...

The cost for the services after you try it may turn off some networkers. In addition, they still need to work through some messaging issues as well as link-backs when they send out e-mails. They also need to add better tutorials to their site for first-time users. Although there is a cost after you test them out, they do offer an affiliate program.

**Straight talk:** If you're looking for these types of customers you should be on this site ...
- Teens and young adults
- Internet-savvy users
- Those looking for dating, relationships
- Online game players

**Another angle: This site could help grow your business if you're in one of the following categories ...**
- Photo or video sharing online
- Targeting teenagers or college students
- Online game developers

## BlitzTime Profiles Consist of ...

**Main picture:** Consider choosing a personal photo for your profile picture, it makes it easier to connect with people and put a face to the person that you're speaking with and vice versa.

**URL:** Your BlitzTime URL isn't based on the name you enter when you sign up. They currently don't offer personalization URLs. They automatically assign you a direct link.

**About me:** Your website, title, location, and resume are automatically displayed. You can write more personal information to share with other users in the info section. You can also upload documents for others to view. Keep your description brief and to the point, but also include why you would be a great person to BlitzTime with and what type of Blitz you are looking for.

People: You can invite people from the main connection page to your event or check out what events they're having and join. People can also request to join your event directly. You can approve or decline them.

## Site Add-ons

**Documents:** You can upload PDFs or Word documents for any user to upload.

**Audio introduction:** You can record an audio segment on your profile to introduce yourself. This is a great way to share what your company does.

**Site customization resources:** There are currently no site customization layouts available.

## Site Marketing and Advertising Opportunities

There are currently no advertising opportunities available for this site. They do offer affiliate programs as you become a paid subscriber and bring other paid subscribers to their network, they will pay you a percentage.

## Getting Started on BlitzTime

Using this guide, you can join BlitzTime, build your profile, and connect with hundreds of potential customers and partners:

- On BlitzTime, click the "Signup" link button and enter the required information.
- Fill out your profile, add your picture, and record your audio introduction.
- Search for Blitztime events and groups that you would like to join and participate in.

# Professional Network Site Reviews

## LinkedIn (linkedin.com)

### What Is It?

LinkedIn is a networking site geared toward the business professional, with the overarching goal of sharing knowledge and tapping into relationships. Your network consists of the people you know: friends, current and former colleagues, schoolmates, industry connections, independent contractors, and more, as well as your contacts' contacts. LinkedIn users can also join groups, and ask and receive answers to industry-specific questions.

### Site Stats

**Born:** May 2003

**Users:** More than 40 million registered users spanning 150 industries, with about 5 million individual visitors monthly

**Demographics:** Almost entirely business executives and owners. Approximately 61 percent male and 38 percent female.

**Cost to join:** Free to join, with two types of account upgrades available—Business, which costs $19.95/month and BusinessPlus, which costs $50/month or $500 yearly.

### Highs: What the site is good at and for ...

Each new connection you make exponentially expands your network by giving instant access to all your new contact's connections. The "Answers" feature is free of charge and potentially more useful to small business owners than the Google or Yahoo! equivalent. The questions asked are typically more business-oriented and the identity of those asking or answering them is known. Entrepreneurs can use the power of the site to increase the relevancy of their job searches, gauge the health of a company or industry, track competitors, and learn more about potential colleagues.

### Lows: What's difficult or missing from the site ...

The "Groups" feature has received criticism for being less than user-friendly, particularly when it comes to administering groups and creating new ones. Extremely protective of members' privacy, it can make adding someone to your network very difficult unless you either know their name and e-mail address or get a referral from an existing friend. No automated way to remove yourself from LinkedIn, you must file a customer support ticket to do so, and it can be unclear that invitation messages are actually sent from the individual whom they claim to be from.

### Straight talk: If you're looking for these types of customers you should be on this site ...

- Employees
- Employers
- Business owners
- Contractors seeking to build their professional networks

### Another angle: This site could help grow your business if you're in one of the following categories ...

- Seeking people to add to your professional network
- Hoping either to hire employees or find a job
- Seeking answers to industry-related questions or wanting to boost your professional profile by answering questions
- Seeking new business relationships by alumni, industry, or professional groups

### Linkedin Profile Consists of ...

**People:** You can search for people in three ways: Advanced Search, Name Search, and Reference Search.

**Jobs:** The "Jobs" function is one of the best-developed parts of the LinkedIn site, providing employers, employees, business owners, and contractors the opportunity to search for and post jobs. This component consists of:

- **Hiring Home:** The central control area for managers, recruiters, or small business owners seeking qualified candidates. General pricing starts at $195 per job listing, but corporate accounts with separate pricing and added services are also available. Since LinkedIn is a social-networking site, posting jobs here rather than other job sites gives employers a major advantage, as their listings will be seen by active job-seekers and those who might be considering a move but haven't yet taken action.

- **Post a Job:** Post a position that is searchable to all 20 million LinkedIn professionals. LinkedIn also offers one-click distribution to your contacts, allowing you to find candidates who come from trusted sources. Searches can be expanded by forwarding your job posting to everyone in your network. If you're not ready to post a job listing, but would still like to put out feelers to your contacts, LinkedIn offers a "Tell Your Network" button that sends an e-mail detailing the general parameters of the job. LinkedIn offers free promotion for job listings exclusively posted on the site. Other Post A Job features include the ability to:
  a. Select only local candidates
  b. Set higher priorities for applicants with recommendations or referrals through your network
  c. Exclude third-party applications

**Manage Jobs:** LinkedIn archives expired job postings, allowing you to view all your current jobs and revisit older postings. Saving drafts here lets you easily change postings and compare responses to differently worded listings. If you're not getting the desired response to a particular listing, you can actively search for candidates using criteria such as name, industry, location, interests, keywords, and network members. Then, when you find someone, a reference search is only a click away.

## Site Add-ons
**Toolbars:**

- **LinkedIn Companion for Firefox 3.0.1:** This plugin for Mozilla's Firefox browser gives you immediate access to your LinkedIn network whenever you're online. You'll be able to see LinkedIn profiles for anyone sending you Web-based e-mail, search your LinkedIn network from any website, bookmark profiles and searches for easy access, and find a job by seeing who in your network can connect you to hiring managers while browsing major online employment sites. Get the plugin at https://addons.mozilla.org/en-US/firefox/addon/1512.

- **LinkedIn Internet Explorer Toolbar:** A plugin similar to the LinkedIn Companion for Firefox. You can download the IE toolbar, as well as a toolbar for Firefox at linkedin.com/static?key = browser_toolbar_download.

- **LinkedIn Outlook Toolbar:** This tool helps you build your LinkedIn network from frequent contacts, manage LinkedIn contacts in Outlook, and receive notifications when your contacts update their LinkedIn profiles. You can also see profiles for everyone who e-mails you and get a notification when frequent e-mail contacts are not in your network.

**Mobile:** Take your LinkedIn to go with this feature, which was launched in February 2008. The Mobile feature includes Blackberry and iPhone users. To ensure the compatibility of your device, log into m.linkedin.com.

**RSS:** As of March 2008, LinkedIn lets members subscribe to network updates via an RSS (Really Simple Syndication) feed. To learn more and to subscribe, visit blog.linkedin.com/blog/2008/03/network updates.html.

## Site Marketing and Advertising Opportunities

As a social network made up almost exclusively of business executives and business owners, LinkedIn offers a powerful means of marketing your products and services. Here are a few ideas to get you started:

**Power Your Profile:** Make your profile a complete, powerful reference tool for potential clients and colleagues. Be certain to add substance, context, and your own voice, as well as recommendations from trustworthy connections.

**Post Your Link to Other Sites:** Add links to your LinkedIn profile to your other social-networking profile pages, as well as to your blog, home page, and other web presences pertinent to your business.

**Join the Community:** Brand yourself and your business by writing recommendations, answering questions, and joining groups.

**Get Listed in the Service Directory:** Become a service provider. Remember, you must first receive a recommendation in order to be listed in the LinkedIn service directory.

**Use Your Recommendations:** Incorporate your LinkedIn recommendations into the resumes you send to potential employers.

**Keep an Eye on Your Contacts:** Keep close watch on your contact list to ensure that your current connections remain relevant, and that no one who should be there is missing.

**Watch the LinkedIn Blog:** Monitor the LinkedIn blog (blog.linkedin .com) to stay abreast of current site news and product releases that may help with your marketing and advertising initiatives.

### Getting Started on LinkedIn:

Follow these steps to launch your own LinkedIn profile and start expanding your business network:
- On LinkedIn, click the "Join Now" button at the bottom.
- Fill in the required information and click the "Join LinkedIn" button at the bottom.

From here you can begin filling in your profile and expanding your business network, along with gaining exposure for your products and services. You have now become a member of LinkedIn. You can find new clients, jobs, employees, and business associates while harnessing the powerful network resources of LinkedIn.

---

# Plaxo (Plaxo.com)

### What Is It?

This free service securely updates and maintains the information in your address book. You can connect with people whom you know and browse the people whom you may know or would like to connect with. They brought the address book feature to life with Plaxo Pulse, a new way to enrich your connection with the people in your life. Pulse is a bit like some social networks you've heard of, but it's different in several key ways. Pulse is not a place to see how many online "friends" you can collect. It's meant to be a better way for you to stay in touch with the people you actually know and care about—your family, your real-world friends, and the people you know from business. Pulse makes it easy for you to see what they're creating and sharing online—their blogs, the photos they're uploading, their restaurant reviews, and more. Pulse just recently became a subsidiary of Comcast Interactive Media. Plaxo remains an independent operation in Silicon Valley.

## Site Stats

**Born:** 2001

**Users:** Plaxo has 20 million active users, Pulse currently hosts address books for more than 40 million people.

**Demographics:** Male and females between 35–64, mainly popular in the U.S.

**Cost to join:** Free

## Highs: What the site is good at and for …

You can hook your Pulse account up to all the places where you create or share stuff (your blog, Flickr, Twitter, Yelp, and more than 30 other sites). Plaxo is not a "walled garden." It's a dashboard for seeing what the people you know are creating and sharing all over the open web. But "open" does not mean "public." With Plaxo, you have fine-grained control over what you share with whom, whether that's your contact info or your photos from last weekend.

## Lows: What's difficult or missing from the site …

There seems to be some talk about Plaxo spamming people's address books when they upload them; however, I couldn't find any data supporting that claim. Plaxo doesn't seem to be as consistent compared to Linkedin. I have found that I can do the same things, actually more on Linkedin. Plaxo is missing the group function, which can be vital in building connections and relationships.

**Straight talk: If you're looking for these types of customers you should be on this site ...**
- Baby boomers
- Connections from your friends and family
- Executives

**Another angle: This site could help your business if you're in one of the following categories ...**
- Seeking to connect with executives
- Seeking to expand your professional network

## A Plaxo Profile Consists of ...

**Main picture:** It's best to upload a professional personal photo, people tend to want to connect more with profiles that have personal photos on this site.

**Connections:** You can connect with people you know by searching their name, e-mail address, or uploading your address book. Currently, Plaxo allows Outlook and AIM upload.

**Pulse Stream:** Post any status updates or information that you want to share with your connections.

**My Photo Albums:** You can create photo albums and upload pictures to your profile for connections to browse through. This is a good way for people to get to know you.

**Address Book:** Once you upload your e-mail database, Plaxo works hard to keep your contacts information current. You can back up your address book and remove duplicates.

**E-cards:** This is a great way to send a personal online note to connections through e-cards. You can even add your own photo to the e-card. There are hundreds of categories and e-cards to choose from.

## Site Add-ons

You can add a Plaxo Badge or Widget to your website or Blogger or Typepad blog. Badges are a customizable way to share your Plaxo information on a website or blog. Your badge will be seen by everyone on the site you post it on (including non-Plaxo users).

## Site Marketing and Advertising Opportunities
Plaxo currently offers Google adword campaigns.

## Getting Started on Plaxo
Follow these steps to launch your own Plaxo profile and start expanding your business network:
- On Plaxo, go to the "sign up now" button.
- After you type in your information, you will have to confirm your account by going to your e-mail and clicking on the verification link.
- Once you verify, go back and set up your profile.
- Upload your address book.

---

# XING (Xing.com)

## What Is It?
XING is global networking for professionals. This site also offers a jobs portal, more than 24,000 expert groups, and networking events from London to Beijing to New York. XING has evolved from a platform to a web interface for business professionals around the world. Known for being a leader in the European market in business networking, XING went public in 2006, the first Web 2.0 company to do so, setting the pace in online business networking. XING AG generated revenues totaling 35.3 million euros in the 2008 financial year, based on a profitable business model incorporating three separate sources of income. Working from the headquarters in Hamburg and subsidiary offices in Beijing, Barcelona, Milan, and Istanbul, XING's staff numbers more than 200.

## Site Stats
**Born:** August 2003
**Users:** More than 7 million active users worldwide
**Demographics:** 40% of Xing users are between the ages of 35 and 49; 57% male users, 43% female; 75% of the users have attended

college and or graduate school.

**Cost to join:** Free for basic membership; Premium memberships start at $5.95/mo.

### Highs: What the site is good at and for ...

The Best Offers section has deals and discounts on everyday purchases. A great site for job searching in Europe. It also has a profile activity meter and it shows the number of people that have previewed your profile as well as who has viewed your profile.

### Lows: What's difficult or missing from the site ...

It becomes difficult to connect with members at the basic level which is free. If you want to connect with certain people in a group and they're premium paying members then you have to upgrade to connect. You can't even set your status as a basic member.

### Straight talk: If you're looking for these types of customers you should be on this site ...

- College students
- Internet-savvy users in Europe
- Recent college graduates beginning their careers
- The 35-and-up crowd
- Executive baby boomers

### Another angle: This site could help grow your business if you're in one of the following categories ...

- Recruiter or head hunter looking for quality job candidates
- Seeking to break into a market in Europe
- Seeking to do more global networking

### A XING Profile Consists of ...

**Main picture:** If you're looking to connect globally a professional personal photo is the way to go. Make sure your picture is clean, easy to see, and sufficiently sized for the space allowed.

**Guest Book:** Check your guest book often to see who is leaving you messages when they visit your profile. If you've set your notification to receive a message when someone visits your guestbook, this is the easiest way to keep in touch with visitors.

**Confirmed Contacts:** As with most networks, you can upload your address book to see if any of your current connections are on this site. You can build your connections from there or start a search and use keywords to find people in specific industries or areas.

**Groups:** Groups are organized in categories of interest such as Art and Culture. It will also show how many groups are under that specific category. Make sure that you check and can speak the language in the group before you join, this site has a large percentage of multi-language users. You can also start your own group.

**Discussion Boards:** The Discussion Board tackles a specific topic raised by principal members of a given group. All members are welcome to discuss this topic.

**Events:** You can create or search and join an event. This section also keeps your own personal calendar. The events section will show how many participants are signed up for the event and how many spots are left. Events will initially come up that match your profile by keyword or you can browse by selected keywords.

**Jobs:** You can search jobs, post, and rate jobs posted by other users. You can post offers that are popular on this site. Each post will have the user's profile next to it.

**About me:** Make sure that you complete and post your About me page live to your site. This can be a brief summary about you and what you do as well as other networks that you are on.

## Site Add-ons

Xing.com plugins are available for free download that allow contact synchronization with Lotus Notes, Microsoft Outlook, Windows Address Book, and Outlook Express. It also allows manual CSV File import–export and has a Firefox search plug-in.

## Site Customization Resources

XING profile pages are standard. There are currently no features or applications available to change individual site profiles. You can customize your profile page under Customization. This section lets you show or make private any area or section of your profile.

### Site Marketing and Advertising Opportunities

Social networking lets you promote your business in a number of creative ways. Here are a few ideas to get you started:

- You can advertise via banner ads on XING by contacting their agency adconion.com/en_us/home/home.html.

### Getting Started on XING

Follow these steps to launch your own XING profile and start expanding your business network:

- On XING, click on the "Sign Up Now for Free" button and enter the requested information. You won't be able to complete your profile setup until you confirm through the link sent to your sign up e-mail address.
- Customize your page and search for connections.

---

# ZoomInfo (zoominfo.com)

### What Is It?

ZoomInfo is a vertical search engine focused on people, companies, and the relationships between them. The site is composed of job-seekers, companies seeking to hire, and businesses looking to sell and market to other businesses. ZoomInfo offers three main searches: People, Companies, and Jobs. They also offer three main services for Recruiting, Sales/Marketing Prospects, and Corporate Research.

### Site Stats

**Born:** Founded as Eliyon Technologies in 2000

**Users:** More than 37 million summaries of business professionals and 3 million company profiles, with nearly 6.5 million unique monthly users

**Demographics:** Very wealthy, slightly female-biased, more educated audience, according to Quantcast. Most users range between 35 and 64 years of age. 30% are mid-level managers or above, and nearly half have an annual income of $75,000 or greater. Nearly all are more than 18 years old.

**Cost to join:** Free. In addition to the free services, they also offer a suite of premium products: ZoomExec ($99/month), PowerSearch (subscription-based), and PowerSell. You'll probably want to upgrade to one of the premium products to take full advantage of the power of the site.

### Highs: What the site is good at and for ...

Simplifying the process of finding people by crawling the web, doing a semantic analysis of web pages, and extracting information to add to its profile database. Building a business by representing yourself or your company, or by creating a company profile. Accessing company information including a general description, annual revenue, and number of employees. Creating your own identity to increase your online exposure.

### Lows: What's difficult or missing from the site ...

ZoomInfo's search engine has been criticized for returning flawed or vague results, as well as outdated information. Getting improved search results typically means signing up for the site's premium services.

### Straight talk: If you're looking for these types of customers you should be on this site ...

- Wealthy, slightly older professionals
- Educated, internet-savvy users
- Job-seekers, companies seeking to hire, and businesses looking to sell and market to other businesses

### Another angle: This site could help grow your business if you're in one of the following categories ...

- Employee recruitment
- A business targeting educated, tech-savvy professionals
- Researching professional and company information

### ZoomInfo Services Consist of ...

**For Recruiters:** ZoomInfo Power Search lets recruiters find high-quality, hard-to-find candidates, some of whom may not even be actively seeking new employment. PowerSearch offers:

- **People Search:** Search for talent using more than 20 parameters.
- **Company Search:** Search for companies by industry, annual revenue, number of employees, geographic region, company ranking, and more.
- **Contact Information:** Find e-mail addresses and phone numbers for candidates.
- **Workflow Management:** Build lists of qualified candidates that you can save and export; share notes on specific candidates with your colleagues.
- **E-mail Campaigns:** Initiate and track high-impact e-mail campaigns to potential candidates.

  ZoomInfo offers recruiters the opportunity to gain access to in-depth profiles on more than 37 million people and to reduce time and resources spent on passive candidates. The site lets recruiters network while looking for top talent.

**For Sales Pros:** ZoomInfo seeks to be a one-stop shop for both sales and marketing prospects. Entrepreneurs in sales can use ZoomInfo to get direct access to the right person in the company they're targeting. That information includes names, titles, and contact information. Those using ZoomInfo for marketing purposes can use the site as a resource for researching companies in key markets, including products and services as well as major executives.

**For Corporate Research:** ZoomInfo has a suite of offerings related to corporate research.

**Company Information:** Accessed by doing a search by company name or keyword. Search by name and ZoomInfo will provide a profile including a general description, industry, annual revenue, number of employees, URL, phone and fax numbers, and lists of key executives and major competitors. Search by keyword and ZoomInfo provides a list of companies that meet your criteria. Click on any of these companies to access their ZoomInfo profiles.

**Accurate Information:** Entrepreneurs and business owners can claim and update their ZoomInfo profiles to increase visibility among potential customers, job-seekers, and other researchers. You can also create or claim your personal ZoomInfo profile to increase your online visibility. Your profile includes information such as career history, education, affiliations, Web references, and contact information.

**Find People:** Search for a person by name, which in turn accesses their ZoomInfo profile and information including current and former employment, education, and online references to show the origin of the information.

**QuickLists:** ZoomInfo lets you keep information on jobs, companies, and potential contacts by saving them here, letting you return to favorite searches at your convenience.

**Business Research:** ZoomInfo offers access to its 37 million people and 3 million company profiles for information on industries, companies, products, services, people, and jobs. Users can receive company and people profiles, ensure the accuracy of their own information, create lists of companies in target industries, find companies that deliver necessary products and services, search for jobs and information on companies of interest, and research competitors or potential partners

## Premium Products
Though joining ZoomInfo is free, we recommend you upgrade to one of the site's premium products to take full advantage of what it has to offer:

**ZoomExec:** For $99 a month, you get access to 1.5 million VP-level executives. This includes:
- **Advanced People Search,** to search for executives by company name, title, location, industry, and company size
- **Contact Information,** for direct contact information for executives
- **People Profiles,** with in-depth information on key contacts, including employment history, education, user-posted biography when available, and references for all information
- **Export Searches:** For an additional 50 cents per name, you

can export your list of executive contacts into your customer-relationship management application for smooth workflow

- **PowerSearch:** An in-depth people search that helps you target your findings with 20 criteria. Also includes
  *Integrated E-mail Tools For Recruiters:* The JobCast e-mail campaign creates, tracks, and sends e-mails to qualified candidates
  *In-Depth Company Search:* Search for companies by industry, annual revenue, number of employees, geographic region, and company ranking
  *Competitor List:* Create a list of competitors to a specific company
  *Networking Opportunities:* Create lists of people similar to those for whom you've searched.
- **PowerSell:** Delivers business intelligence on all levels of professionals and companies. Helps you:
  *Find Decision-makers:* PowerSell's search function lets you seek by name, title, and company to find decision-makers at all levels.
  *Build Your Pipeline:* The application's advanced search functionality lets you create targeted prospect lists by title, geography, company ranking, and company size. Once the list is created, you can also research prospective companies using PowerSell.
  *CRM Integration:* PowerSell lets users export people and company profiles directly into CRM applications to drive more leads.

## Site Add-ons

**Who Is This Person?:** A Firefox add-on that lets you highlight any name on a web page and see corresponding information from sites including ZoomInfo. Get it at https://addons.mozilla.org/en-US/firefox/addon/1912.

**Site customization resources:** ZoomInfo users don't typically customize their profile the way that Facebook and MySpace users do.

You won't see glitter and widgets here, but here are a few ideas for enhancing your own ZoomInfo experience:

- **Complete Information:** Provide complete information on your professional history, including previous employment and education, so that you will be easily found by potential contacts and employers.
- **Subscribe to Premium Products:** To harness the full power of the site, subscribe to one of the three premium products, ZoomExec, PowerSearch, or PowerSell.

## Site Marketing and Advertising Opportunities

Job-seekers, companies looking to hire, and businesses looking to sell and market to other businesses can use ZoomInfo in many ways, including the following:

**Create and Update Web Summaries:** Create and update your own professional or company profile, which gives you control over the information that will be seen by recruiters, job hunters, or potential contacts.

**Advertise on ZoomInfo:** ZoomInfo has begun offering paid advertising opportunities to improve brand visibility. To get started, visit zoominfo.com/about/advertising.

**Access the Right People:** ZoomInfo's search functions allow sales professionals to get direct access to the right person in the company they're targeting, with information including names, titles, and contact information. Marketing professionals can use ZoomInfo to research companies in key markets, including products, services, and major executives.

**Recruitment Tools:** Recruiters on ZoomInfo can find top talent by conducting targeted searches to find professionals in a specific field, whether or not they're active job-seekers. Recruiters can also take advantage of built-in e-mail and workflow management applications.

### Getting Started on ZoomInfo

Follow these steps to launch your own ZoomInfo profile and start expanding your business network:

- On ZoomInfo, click the Register button at the top right corner.
- Fill in the required information.
- Add or edit your ZoomInfo profile, edit your company information, and save your searches into private QuickLists.

---

# Spoke (spoke.com)

### What Is It?

Spoke is a social networking site strictly focused on business. Users can connect with 40 million professionals representing 2.3 million companies. Whether members are looking for employment and promotions or developing new business relationships, the common goal of Spoke members is to grow their business. Software developed by the founders analyzes the strength of member relationships to enhance the connections.

### Site Stats

**Born:** 2003

**Users:** 40 million in 2.3 million companies

**Demographics:** Professionals and executives 35–50 +

**Cost to join:** Free for basic service, with advanced memberships costing $15, $50, or $200 a month

### Highs: What the site is good at and for ...

Connecting like-minded professionals who are looking for a networking community to expand their businesses. Linking small ventures and decision-makers quickly is credited to revving up the process of funding a business. Finding investors to fund your business is easier with a large pool of people who are looking to connect with new businesses.

**Lows: What's difficult or missing from the site ...**
Spoke doesn't currently support Mac OS, Linux, Microsoft Vista, or any e-mail applications other than Outlook. Direct links to profiles aren't available. Some features are limited to paying members, which could hamper opportunities for newer businesses. With so much back scratching going on, it could be difficult to separate reputable businesses from the rest.

Besides a profile photo, the site doesn't use visual media like video and photo galleries. Also, you can't customize profiles.

**Straight talk: If you're looking for these types of customers you should be on this site ...**
- Internet-savvy professionals
- Job searchers, ladder-climbers, and recruiters
- Business researchers
- Marketers

**Another angle: This site could help grow your business if you're in one of the following categories ...**
- Targeting other professionals
- Seeking qualified employees and/or partnerships

## Spoke Profiles Consist of ...

**Main picture:** In this site, individuals can represent companies or you can create a company profile. So when it comes to choosing a main picture, you could choose a logo or a photo of a CEO or another executive to act as a representative. To keep the quality level high, use a professional-grade camera or hire a photographer to take headshots.

**Personal info:** This information is straightforward: your company's name, address, phone number, and website. If your company is a partner or part of a chain, there's also a place to list related companies or groups.

**About me:** Individual profiles function like resumes. You can fill out information about your education, past job experiences, an introduction, etc. Make sure when representing your company that there isn't too much focus on yourself. Be sure to be clear and concise when describing your business.

**Referrals:** Members can promote each other by offering referrals. It's polite to reciprocate when someone recommends you and will help expand and strengthen your network.

**Contacts and Employees:** A company profile will have the list of employees who are also on Spoke, with links to their personal profiles. Contacts are not directly listed on a company's profile; instead there's a tab called "People I Know" where you can see shared connections. Adding people to lists is a premium feature.

### Site Marketing and Advertising Opportunities

Social networking lets you promote your business in a number of creative ways. Here are a few ideas to get you started:

Banner ads: Banner ads are available in two categories: public pages and directories, and members-only. The first group has two available units and can use HTML and Flash, uses targeting, and is "above the fold." The members-only pages offer a skyscraper option in HTML or Flash located "above the fold," visible to business professionals with paid memberships. These are a few companies who can help:

- **My Banner Maker:** mybannermaker.com. Banner creation for many sites
- **Pimp My Profile:** pimp-my-profile.com. Offers an online banner generator as well as customizable layouts
- **MyBannerSpace:** mybannerspace.com. Extended network banner creation with a variety of themes

### Getting Started on Spoke

The following steps will guide you through joining Spoke so you can expand your business network:

- On Spoke, click "Start Connecting Now" to sign up.
- After entering an e-mail address and password, fill out your company information. You will be invited to enter an e-mail address and password to see if your e-mail contacts may already be using Spoke. You'll also be able to search for peo-

ple by name, title, and/or company to begin building a network.

- Fill out your profile, upload a photo or logo, and you're ready to start connecting.

## Insider Tips

Business networking online is just as important as it is in person. So when you get a new business card, add the contact as a connection on Spoke.

Another great way to grow your business is by looking for qualified new hires. Let this be a resource for finding the best of the best.

# Social News and Social Book Marking Site Reviews

## Digg (digg.com)

### What Is It?

A community-driven news and link aggregation site powered by users who vote to promote news items and links. Lets entrepreneurs share information with active communities of potential customers and get noticed if their relevant stories get a larger online vote turnout. Digg is a social bookmarking site that gives the power to the people by allowing them to decide what online news stories, photos, and videos are newsworthy. Members can vote (or "digg") shared content to increase its popularity. Alexa.org ranks Digg in the top 25 websites in the United States. It functions as a one-stop shop for finding the web's best content. A popular link can draw large amounts of traffic to sites, sometimes even causing it to crash.

### Site Stats

**Born:** December 5, 2004

**Users:** Quickly gaining on 3 million users

**Demographics:** 66% are male; 42% are 35 to 49 years old; 26% are 21 to 34 years old; 44% earn $75,000 and above annually; 68% are college-educated or above; 14% are professionals; 10% have an executive or managerial occupation.

**Cost to join:** Free

### Highs: What the site is good at and for ...

Finding and sharing popular news stories, photos, and videos in one place. Shared items are organized into general categories, making it easier to find specific content. Most blogging and news sites have integrated Digg into their platforms, so it's easy to share favorite websites. Also, it's not hard for new users to become familiar with the process. It allows users to connect and discuss on profiles, as well as underneath the shared links.

### Lows: What's difficult or missing from the site ...

It's difficult to promote links that you've shared. Only the most pop-ular make front-page status, so ironically it still takes some digging to get to many of the shared links. It's up to others to make you pop-ular. Users can abuse the democratic system by creating multiple accounts and voting for their own Diggs. Profiles are more of an afterthought, while the focus is on links that take you to other web-sites. Critics say about 25% of the users "control" the front-page content.

### Straight talk: If you're looking for these types of customers you should be on this site ...

- Tech consumers and professionals
- News hounds

### Another angle: This site could help grow your business if you're in one of the following categories ...

- Sharing unique content with many users.

## Digg Profiles Consist of ...

**Main picture:** This photo is linked to your profile, so it would be a perfect place for your logo. Make sure your logo is sufficiently clean and legible for the space allowed.

**URL:** This will be digg.com/users/businessname. To be easily found and identified, try to exactly match your URL to your businesses: digg.com/users/businessname. If your name is already taken, try to add another short identifier, such as your location: digg.com/users/businessnameNYC.

**Favorites:** These are shared items that you've marked as favorites. To the left of these and all shared items is a yellow sticky note—like an image with a number on it that shows its popularity (or how many users "dugg" it).

**Recent Activity:** Like favorites, it shows how you have participated in the site: which items you chose to share, have commented on and which ones you chose to digg.

**About:** A brief space to share a little more about your business and send a message to other users.

**Photos:** This would be good place for photos of products or any other visual elements of your business that could further define your business to users. Keep in mind that all photos are representing your business, so make them good.

Friends: Friends are listed and even show when they were most recently active. There's also a tab that appears on your profile that acts as a feed of all your friends' activity.

**Stats:** Your activity is monitored by:
- Items you've dugg
- Comments you've made
- Items you've submitted
- Your items that were deemed popular
- Your popular ratio
- Friends invited
- Profile views

## Site Add-ons

**Pictures:** Photos are visible to registered members and can be used to give more information about your business. Choose pictures of products, public events, and other representative images.

**Digg the Candidates:** Visibly show support for your favorite presidential candidate through Digg the Candidates. They show up on your profile, and each candidate has a feed to dugg stories about them and the election.

## Site Marketing and Advertising Opportunities

Social bookmarking lets you promote your business in a number of creative ways. Here are a few ideas to get you started:

**Banner ads:** Digg's advertising is run through Microsoft. The skyscraper ad runs on the left side and is tall and narrow (160 pixels wide by 600 pixels tall). Visit advertising.microsoft.com/advertise /digg for creative specs. Try a targeted banner-ad campaign to publicize your services. These are a few companies that can help:

- **My Banner Maker:** mybannermaker.com. Banner creation for many sites.
- **Pimp My Profile:** pimp-my-profile.com. Offers an online banner generator.
- **Style My Profile:** stylemyprofile.net/banner-maker. Custom banner and extended network banner creator that generates, then uploads banners, making it easy for users to cut and paste the embed code.

**Partnerships:** Digg can be integrated into your website by adding some HTML code. It allows readers to participate in Digg while remaining on your site. To download code and learn more about the tools, visit digg.com/partnership.

### Getting Started on Digg

Follow these steps to launch your own Digg profile and start expanding your business network:

- On Digg, click the "Join Digg" button at the top left corner.
- Fill in the required information and click "continue." After verifying your account through a confirmation e-mail, it will ask you to find contacts from e-mail contacts (optional).
- Customize your profile with a photo, a short bio, and links to your website or another online profile.
- Adjust your privacy settings.
- Before you "digg" a link, search for the article, video, or photo in the search bar in the top left.
- If your content isn't found, click Submit New next to the search bar.
- Enter the URL and choose the link's category: news article, video, or image. Some websites allow users to click a Digg logo beneath content to add it to Digg.

### Insider Tips

- The majority of members tend to be online influencers. They are typically educated and professional, so your messaging should be targeted to that psychographic.
- You have to be creative to promote your own site on Digg. So

don't only share links that directly relate to your business, but share ones that would support your message.

- Digg can be used to learn more about what other similar businesses are up.

---

# Delicious (Delicious.com)

## What Is It?

Delicious (formerly del.icio.us, pronounced delicious) is an online social bookmarking website that helps you store, share, and discover new online bookmarks. The visitors to the site can tag their bookmarks in a unique non-hierarchical system that follows the keyword categorizing method. Thus the users can freely select their keywords. You may even get a combined look at the tags available with the bookmarks. For instance if you open a particular URL, you will find all the available tags on one page. Thus you can view all the available bookmarks that have been added by like-minded users. This site has more than 150 million bookmarked URLs.

## Site Stats

**Born:** Late 2003

**Users:** More than 5 million, unquantified traffic data at 318,000 U.S. views monthly

**Demographics:** 51% male; 43% age 35–49; 27% 50 +, 18–34; more Asian visitors here than average; high index of college and advanced college education

**Cost to join:** Free

## Highs: What the site is good at and for ...

Delicious makes it easy to have a single set of bookmarks kept in sync among all your computers; in lieu of having bookmarks on all the computers at which you work. Your bookmarks can be personalized in your collection with custom "tags" or keywords that are then searchable by other users on that topic. This site also has a "hotlist" on its home page, a "popular" and "recent" pages, which helps make the website a conveyor of internet memes and trends. Simple interface, human-readable URL scheme and RSS feeds for web syndication.

### Lows: What's difficult or missing from the site ...
Difficult to search users if you don't know them already. Less focus on users, more on tags and URLs.

### Straight talk: If you're looking for these types of customers you should be on this site ...
- Internet-savvy users
- Recent college graduates beginning their careers
- Male target market

### Another angle: This site could help grow your business if you're in one of the following categories ,,,
- Content-based business
- Author or writer
- Magazine or content producer

### A Delicious Profile Consists of ...
**Network:** Your network connects you to other Delicious users: friends, family, co-workers, even new people you run across while exploring Delicious. It's a "people aggregator," collecting your favorite users' latest bookmarks in one place for you to view and enjoy. You can view and manage your network by going to your Network.

**Fans:** Your fans are a list of people that you add to your network. You can add people to your network and keep track of their latest bookmarks and share your bookmarks with them.

**Bookmarks:** There are several ways to add a bookmark in Delicious. The recommended way is to use one of their browser add-ons. You can also use a bookmarklet on the bookmarklet page. These are simple buttons that go on your bookmarks toolbar. You can also manually create a bookmark by clicking "Save a new bookmark" on the top right of most pages.

**Tags:** These are one-word descriptors that you can assign to your bookmarks to organize and remember them. You choose them yourself and they don't form a hierarchy. You can assign as many tags to a bookmark as you like and you can always rename or delete the tags later. So tagging can be a lot easier and more flexible than fitting your information into preconceived categories or folders.

**Example from Delicious:** If you save an article about how to make a cake, you can tag it with recipes, sweets, yogurt, or whatever other tags you might use to find it again. You don't have to rely on the designer of a system to provide you with a category for French cake recipes. You make up tags as you need them, and use the tags that make the most sense to you.

**Public Profile:** Your public profile is optional information displayed on your Bookmarks page. Creating a public profile lets you personalize your bookmarks and lets other users know who you are. You can also provide ways for people to contact you (via e-mail) or learn more about you (via a website).

## Site Add-ons

The Delicious Bookmarks Add-on enhances your existing Firefox bookmarking system with a new set of tools to help you create, manage, and search your bookmarks. After you download, all of your bookmarks will be instantly accessible both in your Firefox browser and from your bookmarks page on the Delicious website. This means that any changes you make to your bookmarks in either location will be synchronized. For example, adding or deleting a Delicious bookmark in Firefox will add or delete it from your bookmarks page on Delicious. To install visit delicious.com/help/installff.

## Site Customization Resources

Delicious profile pages are standard. There are currently no features or applications available to change individual site profiles. Profiles are brief on this site.

### Site Marketing and Advertising Opportunities
This site doesn't currently offer advertising opportunities as it's a content-based site.

### Getting Started on Delicious
Follow these steps to launch your Delicious profile and start expanding your business network:

- On Delicious, click on the "Join Now" button and enter the requested information. You won't be able to complete your profile set up until you confirm through the link sent to your sign-up e-mail address.
- Enter requested profile information and set up your tags and bookmarks as well as search for fans to connect with who may have the same content interests.

---

# StumbleUpon (StumbleUpon.com)

### What Is It?
StumbleUpon helps you discover and share great websites. This site delivers high-quality pages matched to your personal preferences. These pages have been explicitly recommended by your friends or one of the millions of other websurfers with interests similar to yours. Rating these sites you like with a thumbs up automatically shares them with like-minded people—and helps you discover great sites your friends recommend. When you stumble, you will only see pages that friends and like-minded stumblers have recommended. This helps you discover great content you probably wouldn't find using a search engine.

### Site Stats
**Born:** Late 2001
**Users:** More than 7 million users
**Demographics:** 60% male; 40% age 35–49; most users are in the 18–24 or 35–44 range
**Cost to join:** Free

### Highs: What the site is good at and for ...

This site offers nearly 500 topics among which users may choose to indicate their interests and preferences so each Stumble produces only the most relevant content. StumbleUpon delivers increasingly relevant content as the Toolbar learns what the user has liked in the past and continues to present quality websites in the future.

### Lows: What's difficult or missing from the site ...

Difficult to search users if you don't know them already. Less focus on users, more on content and URLs. This site has also been known to have hardcore pornography pop up on stumbles.

### Straight talk: If you're looking for these types of customers you should be on this site ...

- Internet-savvy users
- Recent college graduates beginning their careers

### Another angle: This site could help grow your business if you're in one of the following categories ...

- Content-based business
- Author or writer
- Magazine or content producer

### A StumbleUpon Profile Consists of ...

**Friends:** You can find friends whom you already know or browse stumblers. The more people you connect with, the more interesting stumble sites you'll receive.

**Groups:** You can view and join groups as well as start and join in on discussions. This site offers a suggested groups list for you, as well.

**Favorites:** You can save your favorite sites and access them from anywhere. Give a thumbs up if you like it and it'll automatically be saved for you. Your favorites can be photos, videos, or discoveries.

**What's New:** Stay up to date on your friends' favorites and reviews. You can also subscribe to a friend's favorite categories if you're interested in the same type of sites.

### Site Add-ons

Add-ons extend Firefox, letting you personalize your browsing experience. Take a look around and make Firefox your own. You can automatically download this from the site.

### Site Customization Resources

StumbleUpon profile pages are standard. There are currently no features or applications available to change individual site profiles. Profiles are brief as this is a content- and URL-driven site.

### Site Marketing and Advertising Opportunities

StumbleUpon will bring people directly to your site. Visit stumbleupon.com/ads/ for more information.

### Getting Started on StumbleUpon

Follow these steps to launch your own StumbleUpon profile and start expanding your business network:

- On StumbleUpon, click on the "Join Now" button, enter the requested information. It will automatically prompt you to download and you want to click Run twice. It will not allow you to have Internet Explorer open during this process so you will need to reopen it once the download is complete.
- You can enter requested profile information and then start searching for friends and stumblers to connect with and share site stumbles.

# Forum Site Reviews

## Meetup (meetup.com)

### What Is It?

Meetup exists to get like-minded people together—online and in their geographical area. The site has seemed to plateau since its popularity drastically increased from 2002 to 2004. Founders Scott Heiferman, Matt Meeker, and Peter Kamali came up with the site after a Harvard sociologist published *Bowling Alone,* which commented on Americans not knowing their neighbors anymore. The site encourages its users to band together to make friends and make a difference.

### Site Stats

**Born:** 2002

**Users:** Averages 1.5 million unique visitors each month, with 52% described as regulars and 32% as addicts

**Demographics:** Most users are ages 25–44, with 60% female users

**Cost to join:** Free, but fees apply for members who post events and serve as organizers

### Highs: What the site is good at and for ...

Joining people together, both on- and offline, by geographical area and interest. Using the internet to encourage personal, face-to-face communication. Rounding up campaign support. RSVP and calendar system make it easy to plan events.

### Lows: What's difficult or missing from the site ...

Some opposed charging for organizers to post events, which began in 2005. Has removed groups without warning. Since these changes, the numbers of users has dropped. However, some say it leads to a more solid and trustworthy user experience. Profiles aren't customizable and don't use video. Personal URLs aren't available and usernames aren't exclusive; you can use your name or a nickname. Advertising is done through Google Ads.

**Straight talk: If you're looking for these types of customers you should be on this site ...**
- Adults
- Internet-savvy users
- Political gurus
- People passionate about hobbies

**Another angle: This site could help grow your business if you're in one of the following categories ...**
- An events-based business
- Targeting specific geographical areas
- Hobby, specific-interest focused

## A Meetup Profile Services Consist of ...

**Main picture:** Your main photo represents you on a profile page as well as when you post comments and appear elsewhere on the site. Small businesses would benefit from using this space for a logo. Something to visually represent your business—a signature product or storefront—may also be appropriate.

**Meetups:** Meetups (or groups) you belong to or have created show up under the "Meetups" tab on your profile. A group profile can also be found through someone searching in your area or topic. This is the bulk of the site and includes many features like a calendar, group rating, number of members, etc. To the left of the profile page, you'll find more tabs that lead you to more about the group: photos, messages, calendar, polls, and more—depending on what the group's organizers have provided. It's highly recommended that you create a Meetup for your business that includes a full calendar, contact information, and bolstering comments section. Give the group a to-the-point name, upload photos of events, and make it as interactive and updated as possible.

**Personal info:** The only other personal information listed, besides your chosen name, is your location. If your company has several locations, you may want to open an account for each location.

**Friends:** The "Friends" tab on your profile lists both those you chose as friends and those who call you a friend.

**Shouts:** Like comments, you can give a shout to someone. This will show up on your profile, so make sure to edit these to ensure your company's image is not compromised. If someone "shouts" you, consider reciprocating to build a relationship.

**Calendar:** This shows up under a Meetups page and is updated by organizers. It functions like an electronic invitation, complete with RSVP and who, what, where, and when information.

### Site Add-ons
**Pictures:** Users are allowed more than one photo, so use this feature to show what your business is about.

### Site Marketing and Advertising Opportunities
Social networking lets you promote your business in a number of creative ways. Here are a few ideas to get you started:

**Groups:** Establishing groups that meet online and face-to-face is the purpose of the site. If your business doesn't regularly host events, consider hosting meetups to get people through your door, and/or for passionate, like-minded people to be excited about your products and services. With thousands of groups across many topics, consider starting several groups. Keep groups updated with photos, user testimonials, events, and activities. Initially you'll work to get people to join the group, and then you'll focus on developing relationships and keeping those members there and excited. To get started, click "Start a Meetup."

### Getting Started on Meetup
Follow these steps to build a personal and group profile page:
- On Meetup, click the "Sign Up" link on the top right of the page.
- Fill out the required information. You'll then be asked to upload a photo and provide other information.
- Next, you'll want to search for Meetups (or groups) by clicking either of these tabs: "Meetups by City," "Meetups by Topic." Small businesses would mostly benefit from creating their own meetups. This can be done by clicking the "Start a

Meetup" tab.

- You'll be asked a series of questions to make sure your group is organized in the best possible place.

## Insider Tips

- Because users have to search for your meetup, it would be a good idea to market your meetup page through other websites.
- A strong profile picture that clearly depicts what the group is about will encourage visitors to learn more about your meetup.
- Businesses not based in a specific location can still throw parties and events. Make plans at a restaurant, bar, or park in various areas—so people throughout the region can feel connected. Make people happy with food, drinks, and activities.
- Consider partnering with other businesses for joint parties. You could even partner with a charity and make the event a benefit or fundraiser.

---

# Craigslist (craigslist.org)

## What Is It?

Launched in San Francisco in 1995, this nonprofit is considered the ultimate site for classified listings, offering ads for jobs, personals, cars, pets, home supplies, and a plethora of other choices. Craigslist is built around communities, with sites now offered in 450 cities worldwide. Though financial information is not disclosed, experts believe Craigslist is worth more than $10 million. A useful means for entrepreneurs to advertise their services and join forums of potential customers free of charge. Corporate headquarters are located in San Francisco. eBay acquired 25% of the equity in Craigslist from a former shareholder in 2004.

## Site Stats

**Born:** Began in 1993 as a series of e-mails, sent to friends, about local events in the San Francisco Bay Area

**Users:** The site serves over 9 billion page views per month world-wide

**Demographics:** Mixed male/female; 45% aged 18–34; 37% aged 35–49; there is a high index of college graduates here.

**Cost to join:** Most posts are free, except $75 per ad for the San Francisco Bay Area; $25 per ad for New York, Los Angeles, San Diego, Boston, Seattle, Washington, DC, Chicago, and Portland, OR; paid jobs and paid broker apartment listings in New York City ($10 per ad); a $5 charge per erotic services listing was added in 2008.

### Highs: What the site is good at and for ...

Real classifieds without too much visual clutter on the pages; straight text. Worldwide exposure and you can search by location.

### Lows: What's difficult or missing from the site ...

There's no real HTML input for ads, the full text-based interface is sometimes hard to navigate in detail.

### Straight talk: If you're looking for these types of customers you should be on this site ...

- College students or graduates beginning their careers
- Customers looking to purchase or trade goods

### Another angle: This site could help grow your business if you're in one of the following categories ...

- Purchase or sale of goods, products, and services
- Recruiting or head hunting

### A Craigslist profile consists of ...

**Posts:** You can post products or services in classified categories on this site. Each post allows you to upload four photos.

**Discussion forums:** You can start or join a discussion forum in many topic areas including the personals romance section.

**Resumes:** You can post your experience on a resume for public viewing on the site.

**Events calendar:** Events are posted in your area in the events section. You can check the calendar for happenings around you.

Jobs: This option allows you to scan and reply/apply for a job in specific categories.

## Site Add-ons

This is a text-based sites. There are no add-ons currently available.

## Site Marketing and Advertising Opportunities

Craigslist is a classified advertising–driven site. You can post in hundreds of categories either selling a product or service.

### Getting Started on Craigslist

Follow these steps to launch your own Craigslist profile and start selling your products and services.

- On Craigslist, click on the "My Account" button.
- Enter the requested information.
- You will need to verify your account on the link sent directly to your e-mail sign-up address before you can start posting on Craigslist.

# Business Directory Site Reviews
## Yelp (yelp.com)

### What Is It?

User-generated reviews and recommendations of restaurants, shopping, nightlife, entertainment, services, and more. Covers specific U.S. cities. Small business owners can buy enhanced profile pages and slideshows that offer more information than regular listings. Yelp provides a directory of businesses in most metro areas and allows registered users to rate and review them. The San Francisco–based company was founded by Jeremy Stoppelman, former VP of engineering at PayPal, and Russel Simmons, lead software architect at PayPal. Perhaps the biggest draw to the site is the open and honest communication; it gives power to the people as well as direct feedback to businesses.

### Site Stats

**Born:** October 2004

**Users:** Compete.com says the site counts about 10 million unique visitors each month; 270,000 business represented as of July 2007.

**Demographics:** 87% of visitors occasionally use the site; 13% visit often; 57% of visitors are women; 19% of visitors are ages 18–24; 28% of visitors are ages 25–34.

**Cost to join:** Free

### Highs: What the site is good at and for ...

Providing a forum for customers to provide feedback on businesses without pressure from advertisers or executives. Maintaining a directory of services, searchable by area. Fostering community, especially between users in the same city or region, as people can message each other, talk in forums, and participate in events. Business pages are easy to print in case you want to take them with you.

### Lows: What's difficult or missing from the site ...

Critics have complained that users aren't necessarily qualified to review, and it leads to an elitist mentality with customers. An Oakland cafe even has a sign displaying "No Yelpers." The Yelp

sponsorship program allows businesses to pay for premier placement in the listings. Some consider this to be misleading and uneth-
ical. It makes the directory organization inefficient: it isn't alphabet-
ical, it isn't by rating, or by exact region. Their mobile version is
fairly weak.

Users can't currently upload video. Businesses don't have much
control over what appears on their page.

**Straight talk: If you're looking for these types of customers you
should be on this site …**

- Educated young adults
- Internet-savvy users
- Foodies
- Shoppers, spa-goers, and nightlife-lovers

**Another angle: This site could help grow your business if you're
in one of the following categories …**

- A store-front service, such as a restaurant or nail salon
- Businesses in metro regions
- A freelancer/consultant running a well-established business

## Yelp Business Pages Consist of …

**Main picture:** Small businesses can benefit from including photos of
their shops to go along with their listing. The first photo could show
up in the directory (depends on the site's placement), so make sure
it's a striking and enticing to draw people in to learn more. A logo
could also go here, too, but it will be less effective.

**URL:** Most often, reviewers will add your business before you do. You
can talk with people at Yelp directly if information they've submitted
is incorrect. More than likely, the link to your business page will be
yelp.com/biz/business-name-location. If you were the restaurant at
Wente Vineyards, the link would be yelp.com/biz/the-restaurant-
wente-vineyards-livermore. If you've set up an account to be a reviewer, you reviewer profile will have the link of yourname.yelp.com.

**Categories:** Another way for people to find your business profile is
through a category. A spa could be listed in categories like skin care,

day spas, and hair removal. Being accurate is key, as it could hurt reviews for a restaurant that closes at 8 p.m. to be listed under Nightlife.

**Contact Info:** Here you would list your address, website, phone number, hours, and other key information. While the other informational items—like parking, price ranges, by appointment only, etc.—may not apply to your business, be sure to enter what you can.

**Message from the Business:** To provide a balance between the company and its reviews, Yelp offers a chance for the company to address site visitors explaining what the business is about. To do this, "claim" your business by clicking "Is this your business?" on the business page.

**Map:** A Google map of your business location is located at the top left of the page. However, those without a brick-and-mortar location will not have a map included.

**Site Reviews:** The bulk of the page will be reviews for your business. In addition to writing, each reviewer is required to rate your business from one to five stars, which will be averaged to create your overall rating. Reviews can be judged by visitors to the site. They can decide if a review is useful, funny, or cool; reviews are also bookmarked, e-mailed, and linked. You can't edit the reviews, but you can contact the reviewer and gather feedback to improve your business.

**Related Searches:** In the sidebar next to the reviews are links to other businesses. You can search for nearby businesses, what people also viewed, related lists, and what's hot and new.

## Site Add-ons
**Pictures:** Anyone can upload pictures of your business, so post professional shots of all that you offer. If you're a restaurant, take photos of gourmet dishes, tables with a glowing ambiance, and people enjoying themselves. Whatever your business, consider this area to be where you can make your services shine. And as always—make sure the photos you choose maintain the image you want to reflect.

## Site Marketing and Advertising Opportunities

Social networking lets you promote your business in a number of creative ways. Here are a few ideas to get you started:

**Featured Review:** In a shaded area atop reviews, you'll find a featured review. It shows up on related business pages like an ad, except it's not an image. Instead, it has a link to your Yelp review page, and includes your overall rating.

**Sponsorship:** You can enhance your business page by participating in the Yelp sponsorship program. It places your business at or near the top of the directory listings, so people will be sure to find you easily. It also includes a bigger slideshow of images placed on the business page, room for announcements of upcoming events or specials, and the ability to feature your favorite review.

## Getting Started on Yelp

- Whether your business is already on Yelp with reviews and ratings or is missing from the directory, it's time to claim your business and sign up for a Business Owner Account 1.
- If you currently have a business with reviews, click "Is this your business?" link under the contact information. Otherwise, go to biz.yelp.com and click "Get Business Owner Account."
- Fill out the necessary information. Yelp will contact you by phone to confirm your account. You'll be granted the ability to access reviewers, add photos to your site and more.

## Insider Tips

- As a business, it's easy to feel crushed by a negative review, but don't let it get to you. People want varied opinions and even the best of businesses are criticized. If you choose to contact the reviewers, it may hurt your business more to blast them. Thank them for taking the time to review and ensure you're taking their suggestions to heart.
- Professional photos are key to convincing readers. Don't skimp on these—it pays to have high-quality artwork online.

- Yelp doesn't have all the answers, so make sure you have a strong website to complete a positive online experience.
- Accurate information is important. It may be tempting to put your business at a lower price point, for example, but if people pay much more than they expect, it could lead to a negative review.

---

# Citysearch (citysearch.com)

## What Is It?

Reviews and directions for top restaurants, events, nightclubs, shops, services, and more, in cities across the U.S. In 2007, CitySearch expanded local business coverage by acquiring InsiderPages.com, which offers user-generated reviews similar to Yelp. Looking for something to do nearby? Citysearch serves as a local directory of everything from art galleries to wedding services. Under parent company IAC (InterActiveCorp), it has acquired Microsoft's sidewalk.com and insiderpages.com.

## Site Stats

**Born:** 1995

**Users:** 14.5 million business listings, more than 600,000 user reviews, ratings on more than 2 million businesses

**Demographics:** The site mainly focuses on restaurants and nightlife, so its users and visitors are typically young adults from 18 to 30

**Cost to join:** Free

## Highs: What the site is good at and for . . .

- Finding top-rated businesses and services in your area
- Integrating photos and videos into business profiles
- Allowing users to provide feedback and rate each listing

## Lows: What's difficult or missing from the site . . .

- Some have complained that the ratings and "best of" categories are easily compromised, leading to general distrust of the review system.

- Listings for businesses aren't as strong in more suburban areas.
- The site design doesn't give prominent position to reviews and may take some scrolling and clicking to find out more information.
- Your profile and link are not customizable.
- The links are too long to share by name (use a URL snipping service like tinyurl.com).

**Straight talk: If you're looking for these types of customers you should be on this site ...**
- Foodies
- Internet-savvy users
- Bar and club hoppers
- Event planners
- Shoppers

**Another angle: This site could help grow your business if you're in one of the following categories ...**
- Restaurant and/or food service
- Brick-and-mortar shop in a metro area
- Specialty service

## Citysearch Profiles Consist of ...

**Main picture:** Entice readers to choose your business by putting photos of a storefront, gourmet dish, or cozy cafe nook. It's recommended that photos are shot professionally (or with professional-quality cameras) to ensure the best first impression.

**URL:** Citysearch URLs aren't customizable and are fairly long. For example, your Oakland-based business would be: eastbay.citysearch.com/profile/numbers/oakland_ca/your_business.html. So it's not likely you'll advertise the link in text, but it's still worth it to link to it from your website.

**Message:** A premium business account allows you to send a message to your potential customers. It's a good place to briefly tell why your business is the best and they should give you a shot. Be sure to clearly highlight what sets you apart from others.

**Contact Info**: Your profile will include your address, phone number, cross streets, and hours. There are also links to a map, printable view, website, menu, e-mail to a friend, send to phone, e-mail the business, and save the site. More information can be found on the right sidebar as well, including parking, payment types, cuisines, and amenities. Not all of these categories will apply, but similar information for your business type is available.

**Editor's Review:** This is where Citysearch employees give their input on what your business has to offer. It is located at the top, above the user reviews.

## Insider Tips

These hints are written by users to provide extra help to first-time visitors. The tips can range from where to park, the busiest hours, and to special offers.

## Site Add-ons

**Pictures:** As a premium business member, you can add a slideshow of photos to show off your business alongside your message. Remember, professional-quality photos are invaluable as people often base their decisions on these first impressions. As a small business, you might want to display shots of product offerings, significant clients, or appropriate personal photos.

**Video:** Premium business members can add video to their business pages. Again, professional quality makes the difference (e.g., well-shot, well-edited video of people enjoying a clean facility).

## Site Marketing and Advertising Opportunities

There are several options to have your business stand out from the rest on these review sites. Here are a few ideas to get you started:

**Banner ads:** Try a targeted banner-ad campaign to publicize your services. These are a few companies who can help:

- **My Banner Maker:** mybannermaker.com. Banner creation for a multitude of sites
- **Banner Sketch:** bannersketch.com. Create an ad with various themes and photos

**Premium Business Member:** Becoming a premium business member gives you the opportunity to have good placement on other websites, as well as video and photo slideshows on your profile page. There are two packages available, Performance and Basic. These can even include professionally shot and edited video.

Getting started on Citysearch: There are two types of memberships to join on Citysearch. One is for people who want to review businesses. The other is for the businesses themselves to help grow their client base. On selfenroll.citysearch.com/welcome.do, you can research the elements of each package to enhance your business profile.

Once you're ready to sign up, click the yellow "Sign Up" button on the top right corner.

If you'd like to learn more about the fees and details, call 1-866-649-1055 or fill out the form under the "Contact Us" tab.

## Insider Tips

- Be brief and accurate in describing your business.
- Mention promotions you have and other incentives to get people interested in checking out your business. Update often.
- While adding information is like an ad, keep the ad lingo to a minimum. Online communication is about connecting people without bombarding them with advertising.
- Professional photos and videos can help your business stand out from the rest.

# Photo & Video Sharing Site Reviews
## YouTube (youtube.com)

### What Is It?

YouTube is a video sharing website where users can upload, view, and share video clips. The technology allows a universe of user-produced video content including movie clips, TV clips, and music videos, as well as amateur content such as video blogging and short, original videos. Unregistered users can watch the videos, while registered users are permitted to upload an unlimited number of videos. Accounts of registered users are called channels. Some content is provided by media networks though the majority is individuals.

### Site Stats

**Born:** February 2005

**Users:** Reaches over 81 million people in the U.S. monthly

**Demographics:** Mixed male/female, teens through adults; there's a high index of people with no college here

**Cost to join:** Free, must register to upload videos and keep a channel

### Highs: What's the site good at and for ...

- Free video hosting
- The ability to feature your own channel of content, managed, and promoted to tailor your message

### Lows: What's difficult or missing from the site ...

- Quality of video compression degrades with size. Without focus, your video can be lost in a universe of other content. Greater chance of duplicate themed content. No blocking anything here; you upload, you show.

### Straight talk: If you're looking for these types of customers you should be on this site ...

- College students or graduates beginning their careers
- Teenagers

- Internet Savvy users

**Another angle: This site could help grow your business if you're in one of the following categories ...**
- Content or information
- Viral marketing or promotions

## A YouTube Profile Consists of ...

**Photo:** You can upload a photo to your profile. We recommend uploading a fun yet professional photo of yourself to your site profile.

**Videos:** You can upload and post videos that you create or have permission to use. If you have music on your video, make sure you have the rights to use it.

**Playlists:** This is a great way to categorize your favorite videos.

**Subscriptions:** These are videos or users that you want to subscribe to. This way you can keep in touch with them and view videos that they post.

**Channels:** You can browse and or post videos on one of the many topic-specific channels such as comedy, how to, or entertainment. You can also create your own channel and name-specific URL.

**Community:** In this section you'll find contests, events, and groups.

## Site Add-ons:
- The YouTube APIs and Tools let you integrate YouTube's video content and functionality into your website, software application, or device.
- The Data API allows a program to perform many of the operations available on the YouTube website. It's possible to search for videos, retrieve standard feeds, and see related content. A program can also authenticate as a user to upload videos, modify user playlists, and more. Visit this link for more information or to set up: code.google.com/apis/youtube/getting_started .html#data_api.
- Custom players and widgets are also available to enhance your YouTube experience.

### Site Customization Resources

There are currently no features or applications available to change individual site profiles on YouTube.

### Site Marketing and Advertising Opportunities

Broadcast your campaign on YouTube. For specific advertising opportunities, contact youtube.com/t/advertising.

### Getting Started on YouTube

Follow these steps to launch your own YouTube profile and start broadcasting yourself.

- On YouTube, click on the "Sign Up" button.
- Enter the requested information.
- You must find a username that is not already in use.
- You will need to verify your account on the link sent directly to your e-mail sign up address before you can start broadcasting on YouTube.

---

# Flickr (Flickr.com)

### What Is It?

An online photo management and sharing application. For less than $25 annually, you can upload an unlimited number of photos, which can enhance your small-business profile. Flickr also offers video sharing. Uploading your files to Flickr interest groups can improve brand awareness. Flickr is currently owned by Yahoo!.

### Site Stats

**Born:** February 2004
**Users:** Over 24.1 million users
**Demographics:** 54% male; 46% female; over 61% have no kids
**Cost to join:** Free for basic users, must register to upload and organize photos

### Highs: What is the site good at and for ...

A clean site, easy to navigate and get familiar with how to use. Free photo and video hosting for basic users.

## Lows: What's difficult or missing from the site ...
Quality of photo resolution and video compression degrades with size. Without focus, your video can be lost in a universe of other content.

## Straight talk: If you're looking for these types of customers you should be on this site ...
- College students or graduates beginning their careers
- Internet-savvy users

## Another angle: This site could help grow your business if you're in one of the following categories ...
- Content or information
- Viral marketing or promotions
- Photography- or portfolio-based

## A Flickr Profile Consists of ...
**Upload:** Upload photos from your desktop, send by e-mail, or use your camera phone.

**Edit:** Get rid of red eye, crop a photo, or get creative with fonts and effects.

**Organize:** Use collections, sets, and tags to organize your photos and videos.

**Share:** Use groups and privacy controls to share your photos and videos.

**Maps:** Share *where* your photos and videos were taken, and see photos and videos taken near you.

**Make Stuff:** Sexy cards, photo books, framed prints, Target pick up, DVDs, etc.

**Keep in Touch:** Get updates from family and friends.

## Site Add-ons
Add-ons extend Firefox, letting you personalize your Flickr experience. Visit addons.mozilla.org/en-US/firefox/addon/4286 to upload.

## Site Customization Resources

There are currently no features or applications available to change individual site profiles on Flickr. However, you can customize your photo sharing features.

## Site Marketing and Advertising Opportunities

Flickr is for personal use only. You have to arrange any commercial use with Flickr first. Click Help by E-mail at the bottom of the page and choose "I have a business proposal."

## Getting Started on Flickr

Follow these steps to launch your own Flickr profile and start sharing your photos.

- On Flickr, click on the Sign Up button, enter the requested information. You will be required to either enter your Yahoo! e-mail account information or set up a new Yahoo! e-mail account.
- You will need to verify your account on the link sent directly to your e-mail sign-up address before you can start posting and sharing photos and videos on Flickr.

# What About All the Other Sites?

So, what about all the other sites that are currently out there? Not to mention the hundreds, possibly even thousands that will be popping up over the next few months and or years to come? My answer is simple: If they are not directly related to your business industry or target market then forget about them ... at least for now.

Choose the top three sites that are best for marketing your services and or products on and focus on them. I do suggest that you give each of these top three sites that you choose a good three to six months before you write them off. Just as it does in person, it takes time to build relationships and credibility. The advantage of being online however is that you can reach out to hundreds, thousands, even millions of new potential customers and or clients at a time.

I have included an additional 15 sites here with a quick brief on what each site is about as defined on Wiki. I also threw in a few definitions from my personal experience.

## Buzznet.com

This is a photo, journal, and video-sharing social media network. Like other social networking sites, Buzznet is a place for members to share content based on their personal interests. Unlike classic social networks, which focus primarily on messaging and profile pages, Buzznet members participate in communities that are created around ideas, events and interests; most predominantly, music, celebrities, and the media.

## MyYearbook.com

This is a social networking site similar to MySpace, Facebook, and Friendster. It was founded by teenagers and aims to bring together teens all over the world. The idea was to create a digital, interactive version of everyone's favorite old yearbook.

## CouchSurfing.com

This is a free, Internet-based, international hospitality service, and it is currently the largest hospitality exchange network. Members use the website to coordinate contacts and home accommodation (or "surf" others' "couches") with other network members around the world. The website allows the creation of extensive profiles, and uses an optional credit card verification system, a personal vouching system, and personal references to increase security and trust between members. The site offers other features such as discussion groups, events and meetings, and live chat.

## Yahoo! 360°

Yahoo! operates this personal communication portal. It is similar to other social networking sites and while text on the site still describes it as being in beta testing, in fact development has ended and the site is no longer actively supported. Long after support ended, the promised replacement social network site has never materialized. 360° includes social networking, blogging, and photo sharing services.

## Netlog

Formerly known as Facebox and Bingbox, this is a Belgian social networking website specifically targeted at the European youth demographic. On Netlog, members can create their own web page, extend their social network, publish their music playlists, share videos, post blogs and join groups called "clans." Clans can be public or private. The biggest private clan on Netlog bears the rather ironic name, The Anti-clans. It is composed of about 4,100 members. Each member can invite friends on his page and thus create a link between his profile and the profile friends. Netlog has also made it possible for companies to create "brand" pages to promote their products/services. A self-advertise platform has also been introduced to allow advertisers to get their adverts out in the open, quicker! Not only can adverts be placed around Netlog, advertisers can also "customize" what members it goes out to by limiting it to the users interests, age, region and many more factors. Netlog has recently converted its clan platform into what is now known as "Groups". This provides the owners of groups to have a much more "controlled" administration of their group.

## Reunion.com

MyLife.com (as of 2009) is a social network service founded in 2002 by Jeffrey Tinsley after meeting his wife at their high school reunion. The company began with the acquisition of high-schoolalumni.com and PlanetAlumni.com. The website claims to help members find and keep in touch with friends, relatives, and lost loves.

## Classmates.com

This is a social network service created in 1995 by Randy Conrads who founded Classmates Online, Inc. The social media website helps members find, connect, and keep in touch with friends and acquaintances from throughout their lives—including kindergarten, primary school, high school, college, work, and the United States military.

## LiveJournal

Often abbreviated LJ, this is a virtual community where Internet users can keep a blog, journal, or diary. LiveJournal's differences from other blogging sites include its well-liked features of a self-contained community and some social networking features similar to other social networking sites.

## ProfileHeaven

Formerly known as Faces.com, this is 95% UK member-based with other countries, prominently users from America and Australia, making up the remainder. The typical demographic to begin with was members between the ages of 16 to 22, mostly females. As many other social networking sites provide, each user can create a profile and blog about themselves. Users can link these profiles together to form a linked friend network. Other notable features are web forums, unlimited photo galleries, video, live video chat, flash games, and a points ranking system.

## Squidoo.com

This is a community website based in Hastings-on-Hudson, New York that allows users to create pages (called lenses) for subjects of interest. Lenses are interactive, and can contain Flickr photos,

Google maps, blogs, eBay auctions, YouTube videos, and other links. Squidoo is in the top 200 most-visited sites in the world, and in the top 50 most viewed in the United States. It is a great site for Authors to create content lens pages to build their credibility and exposure.

## Care2

This is a social network website that was created to help connect activists from around the world. It has a membership of approximately 9 million people. Care2's stated mission is to help people make the world a better place by connecting them with the individuals, organizations, and responsible businesses making an impact.

## Ryze.com

This is a free social networking website designed to link business professionals, particularly new entrepreneurs. The site claims to have over 500,000 members in 200 countries, with over 1,000 external organizations hosting subnetworks on the site. Both paid and unpaid membership levels are offered.

## Goodreads

This is a privately run "social cataloging" website that permits individuals to sign up and register books to create their library catalogs and reading lists. They can also provide rating reviews and feedback on books as well as suggest books to friends. A great site for authors to promote their books and build their reviews.

## Blackplanet.com

This is an online niche social-networking site targeted especially for the African American community. This site seems to have a personal focus rather than a business-building niche.

## Orkut.com

Thi is a free-access social networking service owned and operated by Google. The service is designed to help users meet new friends and maintain existing relationships. Although Orkut is less popular in the United States than competitors Facebook and MySpace, it is one of the most visited websites in India and Brazil.

If you can't seem to find a social networking site for your industry or target market, create one by using a Ning platform as discussed in previous chapter. Be the leader, start a movement, start a social site, and connect people and get them talking about your area of business interest. I have seen Ning sites for communities, cities, government sectors, skydiving, speed flying, ice skating, dancing, yoga, and many more.

# Get Connected Through Article Marketing

Online content is the key to building successful relationships and trust. People connect with you the more they get to know you and if they feel that you are continually offering valuable information, they will do business with you when the need surfaces. Content includes free reports, articles, columns, top tips, resources list, statistic, or studies released and even quotes and comics such as photos and/or comic strips related to your industry.

There are several ways to get your content out over the internet. Post directly to your blog as well as the social networks that you belong to with a link back to your blog. Another way is to release your content onto article marketing sites (aka article directories) that will link back to your site and or blog and also post your credit, as well as reach the masses on their networks. These sites already have a large clientele looking for your articles. Most article marketing sites are free, some you will have to pay for placement. There are a few sites that have to approve your content before it goes live, however, it usually doesn't take longer than 48 hours. I have included a list of article marketing sites in this chapter that I compiled from Google searching, as well as those I use for my own personal and client campaigns.

So how do you create content? The first thing you need to do is create a content map. A content map includes a timeline as to how often you're going to release content, as well as a topic list. If you're not an expert writer or if you have a challenging time putting your thoughts together, then I suggest that you either locate ghost-written articles in your industry or area of interest, and purchase the rights to publish it with your credit. There are hundreds of sites on the internet and many in your industry that you offer this content to you. The fastest way to find them is to either Google "ghost written articles for purchase" or contact your trade or industry organization and ask them if they have any site or writer leads for you.

If you want to have at it yourself, then great. Let's get started. I suggest that you mix up your content with all the suggested content types I mentioned. Maybe one article a month, a few quotes here and there, a top tips post, study release, and maybe a few funny photos to go with some of your content. Ask yourself this: What interests you? Why do you pick up a magazine or newspaper and read an article in your area of interest? Whatever it is that keeps your attention, it will most likely keep your potential customers or clients as well. If you have a contact database list, reach out to them and ask what they read or what they would like to see more of. Regardless of what type of content you create or buy, your content pieces need to encourage, enlighten, and inform! If you incorporate articles, I suggest that you keep your articles at no more than 750 words, no less than 350.

Each of the sites on this list have different submission guidelines and may or may not have fees associated with the posting. I always stick to the free sites, and I've found that I get thousands of visits from one article posted on one site. Article marketing is very effective if you execute it correctly. I posted "Top Five Mistakes People Make with Social Networking" on all the leading free article marketing sites and on my social networks. I received close to 10,000 unique visitors to my site in one week and captured close to 3,000 e-mails to add to my e-mail database. E-mails are golden!

## Top Article Directory Sites

1. businessknowhow.com
2. buzzle.com
3. Ezinearticles.com
4. Goarticles.com
5. selfgrowth.com
6. articlealley.com
7. Articlebase.com
8. articlecity.com
9. articledashboard.com
10. isnare.com

11. websource.net

12. amazines.com

13. article99.com

14. articlebiz.com

15. articleblast.com

16. articlesfactory.com

17. Searchwarp.com

18. promotionworld.com

19. articlesphere.com

20. articletrader.com

21. ideamarketers.com

22. worldwebindex.com

23. excellentguide.com

24. afroarticles.com

25. articlecube.com

**BONUS**—*Two more for you!*

26. selfseo.com

27. contentdesk.com

Now that you have this list, what do you do with it? You take your valuable content that you either purchased or created for your target market, remember some thing different, compelling and uplifting and submit it to at least five of these sites on the list. If you can commit to all 25 great! My personal top five favorites are:

- ezinearticles.com
- goarticles.com
- web-source.net
- articlealley.com
- buzzle.com

**TIP:** For marketing maintenance online send or post content once a month, for marketing magnificence send and post at twice or more per month.

**TIP:** Use RSS feeds to syndicate your articles. RSS stands for Real Simple Syndication. RSS is a great way to get people to subscribe to your content articles. A few examples: Google Blog Search, Microsoft's RSS Powered Longhorn, and XML Sitemaps.

**TIP:** Use autoresponders for your articles and automate your genius. Some top sites for auto responder campaigns are aweber.com or constantcontact.com. Both sites have video tutorials.

**TIP:** Make sure you post your article on your site. I prefer to post to my blog because it allows for interaction and comments with visitors. This is huge for key word traffic from the search engines.

**TIP:** Use affiliates if you have them, if not set a few up. An affiliate would be some one you partner with to share their content and articles to your list and they do the same for you to their list. These should be people in the same industry who aren't competition and you both compliment each other. Example: a nutritionist and a personal trainer.

**TIP:** Place your most popular articles in an eBook that can be branded and shared. This is a great way to get your content go viral on the internet.

**TIP:** Cross reference your articles by placing links to your other articles in the article you're writing. If you're offering helpful advice, most ezine editors and webmasters will let you do this. It's OK to self-promote. No, really, it is.

# Social Networking Case Studies

 The case studies presented here were acquired by the same techniques recommended in this book. We posted in several groups on LinkedIn as well as two tweets on Twitter asking if anyone had social-networking success stories they would like to share. The response was overwhelming. With the help of our assistant, Vanessa Stricklin, we narrowed the list down to about 20 people we wanted to interview. From those 20 interviews we picked the best 10 stories to offer you a variety of experiences from a diverse background. We didn'tt select stories based on the amount of success they had achieved, nor did we choose only those people who were "experts" at social media. Some are experts and some are newbies with only two to six months of social-networking experience. None of the participants were paid for their interviews.

## Case Study 1

### Jim Talerico, Greater Prairie Business Consulting, Dallas/Fort Worth, TX, LinkedIn.com/in/jamesjtalericojr

Talerico used the power of social networking to grow his independent consulting practice in ways he never could have imagined using traditional methods.

Here is Jim Talerico's social-networking story in his own words:

**JT:** I'm 38 years old and I didn't grow up around computer technology, although I wouldn't consider myself backwards, either. My experience is that I was aware of social networking, but really struggled at getting good with it because I saw it as just another thing that would consume my time. I get bombarded with enough e-mail during the day. Why would I want to add something else to manage?

I've been doing consulting for quite awhile, and I was managing a division of a consulting firm in the greater Chicago area. I worked with that company for a couple of years, and I thought it was time for a change and that I wanted to do some stuff on my own. I was on a plane, and I met a young guy who was a consultant. He was helping companies use social networking as a way to grow their sales. We had an intriguing conversation, and I decided to do things on my own. I started with LinkedIn and was pretty aggressive in terms of social networking. In less than six months, I had almost 2,500 LinkedIn contacts! I was looking to use it as a vehicle for helping companies find financing. As a result of doing that, a lot of positive things have happened. I'm in the process of closing some huge deals right now. I've been presented with more business opportunities than I can really try to handle. I am very excited about the future prospects, and although it does involve time, at the same time I've been able to find many new opportunities.

*So was finding financing for companies something you had done for your job before?*

**JT:** I had, but one of the problems was finding the opportunity to finance and on the other end of that it was challenging to find the people who would do the financing. It was a laborious process, unless you had been in this business a long time and had all these contacts. What LinkedIn allowed me to do, because it had specific groups, was quickly identify people for those opportunities.

*So you're actually finding not only the client, but you're finding the investors through LinkedIn, as well?*

**JT:** Yes, both those possibilities exist on Linkedin. I've been working with a limited number of clients, because I only have a limited amount of time in a day. Some of the opportunities I'm working with right now are with former clients, but it was my contacting them to let them know what I was doing and my efforts, in terms of networking, that presented some of those opportunities.

*What's the average amount of financing you're seeking?*

**JT:** It's almost a mind-boggling number. For example, I had a client that was involved with alternative energy, and I think he was just a little bit early. I initially helped him with some seed financing so they could get off the ground, but now the timing for alternative energy opportunities is perfect and they needed more. They needed financing in the hundreds of millions of dollars. What I was able to do was put them in touch with somebody who could provide that funding. In fact, the funding is supposed to happen this week.

Another thing that happened that was really positive, and this is how I connected with Starr, was that the consulting work I had done in the past had been written up in the *Wall Street Journal* and other big publications, and so I connected through LinkedIn with the writer of the *Wall Street Journal* article. She called me up and said, "Hey, I'm doing an article on social networking for the *New York Times*." If you Google it under my name, you can see it. Of course this adds to my credibility.

So now the challenge for me is, "Where's the biggest bang for the buck?" and focusing in on those, because I really have more opportunities than I can seriously pursue. I can sense that if I was reading this, I would think, "OK, whatever. This guy's got all these big connections, and how does this relate to me? I'm just a small-town entrepreneur running this shop or that shop." Yes, I had some prior connections, but my point is I have quadrupled my connections through Linkedin.

My new connections have increased by the thousands. That's a true statement. And one of the other things is, in spite of me having some of these connections, my focus on social networking helped in two areas. Number one, it made me be more conscious of networking. I would think of connecting connections that I already had with people I had met on LinkedIn. It makes me think: Who the heck do I know that can help in this situation or with this deal? Focusing on that made me more aware that there are synergies that are related. What I'm surprised at is, when I looked at LinkedIn, how closely connected we are to other people. Check out two or three levels down, for example that Kevin Bacon thing, knowing this person through a series of different connections, you may know somebody else that you didn't realize you were both connected to.

*So how much of your new business has been generated through your connections on LinkedIn?*

**JT:** Pretty much all of it. It's really where I've been focusing all my energies, I haven't been advertising or doing cold-calling, I've been growing my consulting practice by networking online.

*In the past, was that part of how you built a business—cold calling and advertising?*

**JT:** Yes. I was a stockbroker, and I would get a list and have to call maybe 100 people a day to net a handful of appointments.

*You said you went from zero to 2,500 connections. You were obviously pretty aggressive in making connections. What was your strategy for making new connections?*

**JT:** First, it was tapping into the connections that are new. The vehicle that helped me the most was joining groups. You can join up to 50 different groups and it is good to be primarily networking in those groups. I found people that would be helpful for me on the financing side: venture capitalists, hedge-fund people, and financing people. Consulting was another group of people that I connected with. I networked and built a good number of people with an assured level of expertise.

# Case Study 2:

## Kathy Kelly, of Kathy Kelly Productions, Inc., Central Coast, CA

Creator of the Winery Music Awards (winerymusicawards.com and myspace.com/winerymusicawards)

Kelly used a variety of traditional marketing and social-networking strategies to promote her successful events—gaining over 10,000 visitors from 67 countries in a short six months!

Here is Kathy Kelly's social-networking story in her own words:

**KK:** The Winery Music Awards interestingly enough was my brainchild after I had been asked to do some events for a winery after moving to the Central Coast of California. I am a veteran TV producer, marketer, advertiser, and when I moved to the Central Coast, one of the wineries asked me to help them do some events and the first event that they had asked me to do was a Casablanca theme party for a women's shelter. After that the winery owner asked me to do some type of jam session, a music jam session that would help draw people to his winery to help him sell product and basically I said, "Well you are not going to get artists to play for free. So why don't we come up with an idea for maybe a contest?" And with American Idol being such a big hit, I thought to myself this is an opportunity to create something specifically to attract the youngest or the fastest growing demographic, wine-consuming demographic, which is 21- to 34-year-olds, by using music and making it a competition. And so in determining what kind of music and how it could work, we decided not to go with the traditional just jazz, and open it up to all types of music that wine-consuming audiences would like and that includes a lot, from rock to alternative to country to everything except for rap and grunge. We wanted to give access to independent artists that did not have a record deal, who were trying to get the exposure and were willing to play for prizes.

We set it up in the first year and did four shows all at the same winery, the first three shows were the competition and the final narrowed it down to six finalists and then the final show determined first-, second-, and third-place winners. Being from Los Angeles, one of my clients at EMI was leaving and starting his own record label, so he said he would give the winner a record deal, so that kind of worked out pretty well and we got a whole host of other prizes. By the end of the last show, we actually had a complete sellout crowd and it got so busy that we sold standing room only tickets and ended up shooting video to project the show into the standing room area.

With the success of that, we decided to expand it, I revamped the model of the show and expanded it to five shows and moved it from winery to winery to winery. To promote the show, I used a whole host of marketing techniques and tactics to really get the word out there including video and especially social marketing and social networks.

We used commercials, CRTV, which is 30-second and 60-second commercials with an 800 number and a URL website that drove people to buy tickets online. We used radio, posters, postcards, newspapers, magazines, and e-newsletters. We used Google Ad Words, which really helped expand the reach, in fact our Google analytics showed in a six-month period of time, we had over 10,000 visitors from 67 countries.

We did a massive national ePR campaign and it got picked up by bloggers, all sorts of different magazines, and we used links in calendar listings, both in print and online.

After shooting all of the footage, each show was shot with video, and which I used to create segments or videos of each of the performing artists, and we put those on MySpace, Facebook, and YouTube. We also did a live webcast at the finals where we had a two-camera live feed. We basically set up a Winery Music Awards network and people from all over the world could watch the show live from home. When people found out we were doing a live webcast, people in the audience were calling their friends all over the place saying hey, log on, check this out, the word of mouth of that alone as great.

*What was the advantage to have all these people from around the world, if it's primarily a local event. How is the event benefiting from all that viewership?*

**KK:** As we expand the show, it will travel to other wine regions of the world. So in other words, what we did is set up the model in 2007. Now we can take that model and expand into different wine regions around the world. As I continue to build out my network online, it allows me to grow regionally and then internationally.

*Tell me exactly what social-networking sites you used and when you first decided that was going to be part of your plan.*

**KK:** MySpace, Facebook, and YouTube were our main focus. I had to learn how to use them first. Once I did I knew that I had to go on the social-network level, because my budget was so small. It was basically a sponsorship drive that was minimal money, because it was a new event. I also got a little assistance from some younger folks and from people that are already on MySpace and Facebook, and they gave me some basic information on how to make it work and being kind of a computer person myself I just jumped in.

*I've seen a lot of people put a video out on YouTube or they set up a MySpace account and nothing happens, so how did you gain traction with those sites? How did you gain fans and build up your network?*

**KK:** I had an assistant work with me and continue to make friends and continue to scan the internet and build up friends of friends, look at their MySpace page, find out who was on their MySpace page and get similar people that already liked what our brand was about and invite them to be our friend. We would then drive friends to our YouTube videos.

*What would you say the effectiveness of that was relative to the other techniques that you used such as advertising and television? Do you have any sort of tracking as to how well the social-networking part actually contributed to people coming to the show?*

**KK:** I think it shows in our website numbers and attendance that our efforts on social networks paid off. The sites continue to build more friends, and what we are doing builds brand equity. It is a cost-effective, inexpensive way, to continue your marketing efforts on social networks so why not spend a little time, an hour a day continuing to build your network of people, so when you do have the big announcement you are exponentially announcing it to a larger audience.

*Did you engage with anyone who you saw was a key influencer online?*

**KK:** Yes, I hooked up with several people that I know are music and wine lovers and they helped cross promote the brand on their e-newsletter and to their social network of friends. In return, I gave them free tickets to the shows.

*Some readers may have little knowledge of the sites we are talking about like MySpace or Facebook. How would you convince them that social networking is a better way to market their business than the traditional marketing?*

**KK:** Being in marketing and advertising for pretty much my whole life, I have seen the trends and I have seen what we evolved from. The internet is here and now and it is the future of how we will get all of our information. Yes, we there will most likely be print newspapers and lifestyle magazines but even they will have an online presence. The key is, you have to find your own market on the internet.

# Case Study 3:

## Jorge Olson, Liquid Brand Management, Inc. and Cube 17, Inc., San Diego, CA, jorgeolson.com

Olson is an entrepreneur, author, and trainer who has used social networking to not only establish himself as an industry expert but show others the way, as well. He's currently writing a book on the beverage industry called *Build a Beverage Empire* and has self-published another book called *The Unselfish Guide to Self-Promotion*.

Here is Jorge Olson's social-networking story in his own words:

**JO:** I help companies and individuals to market and sell more products. Right now, for me, it is a very busy time, for a lot of people it's slow. One of the things that I have done online is establish myself as a beverage industry expert in the U.S. I've positioned myself as an industry expert for one niche or another on many occasions as well as other people that have hired me. Because of the internet, it's much easier to build a brand and a business or establish yourself as a leader.

I do it with blogs, websites, and social networks primarily. LinkedIn is an example. I created LinkedIn groups for different niches including beverages, which is called a beverage business group. I also have one for writers, one for speakers, and one for exporting your product to Mexico. People who are in the beverage industry from every company in the U.S. and even abroad, even distributors, join my beverage group

175

and start networking with me, asking me questions, and I provide value.

I try to provide as much value as I can online. For example, I write weekly articles on beverages for my blog. I have a blog-talk radio on beverages where I talk about how to start and fill beverages. All of this information that I provide is free. The book, of course, will be sold, but everything else is free. This is the type of content that people are looking for online.

I currently have 10,000 people that have subscribed to my newsletter. They have all signed up through articles and through blog-talk radio or through LinkedIn. This is just my personal database; I am not including LinkedIn that's another 10,000 to 15,000.

It is called a social network, not a selling network. You have to connect with people first.

I get 100 percent of my business through online networking. People read about me in an article or online with a press release or on a social network, then come to my blog and they subscribe to my newsletter and then they call me and they say, "You don't have to sell me. I know what you do. I've read your articles, I feel I know you because I've listened to your recordings. This is my project. What do you think?"

*So, have you stopped traditional advertising all together?*

**JO:** Yes, 100 percent, yes! Not only have I stopped traditional advertising, I have recommended to many of my customers to stop, as well. Everybody who calls me—and, by the way, it's all incoming calls, I don't make outgoing anymore nor do I use direct mail.

*When did you realize that this was where you needed to focus to build your business?*

**JO:** I have a little bit of an advantage because I used to work in software and technology. I used to be an executive for software companies and internet companies about 10 years ago. So, I was on the cutting edge of marketing to colleges and I am an early adapter. By the time I was about 27 years old, I was VP of marketing for a software company and about 10 years ago is when all of this started.

Back then, this type of technology was very expensive. I know, I used to sell collaboration software for $200,000 to $2 million. The companies that could afford it, my customers, were Chevron, Schlumberger, United Nations, and other big *Fortune* 100 companies. The same technology that I was selling 10 years ago is what we call now social networking and it's free.

*A lot of small businesses that aren't using social networking as a daily part of their marketing and branding are not really seeing the value because they still see it as something that their kids do. Why is this type of perception hurting them?*

**JO:** The power is in the people you can connect with. The amount of people that you can connect with online is unlimited. Why would you not want to tap into that? I have close to 7,000 people on my Linkedin account alone and I've been in it just a couple of months. How could I interact with 7,000 people in person? I don't even think I could handle 70.

*How can a business build thousands of contacts in just a few months?*

**JO:** It's very simple, there are just a few key steps that you have to follow. First of all, you have to complete your network profile. This includes a photograph of you, not of your dog or your pet or your kid or your logo. People who are savvy networkers will not network with you if they can't see your photo, they don't take you seriously.

Secondly, you have to be an open networker. You must accept invitations from anybody, not just people that you know. Most people are very shy when they start to do that, and they only want to connect with the 30 or 40 people they already have a relationship with, but that defeats the purpose. You don't need LinkedIn or Facebook for that. You already know them and that's not what we're talking about—we're talking about business. So, be an open networker, and that means I allow invitations.

*As soon as businesses build their networks, what's next?*

**JO:** The purpose of being online and using software is automation. If it's not automated, it doesn't make any sense. One thing that will help with automation is to join groups of interest on your social-networking sites. In addition, there are a lot of free software clients that will help you set up automation for your social-networking campaigns.

In addition, you have to send your new contacts and connections somewhere; send them to your website or to a blog. This is how you actually take advantage of these networks, when they land on your site. They are interested and they will explore further and possibly purchase your product or inquire about your services. Hopefully your site has a blog so that it is interactive and it will need to have some value, how-to articles or top tips.

I recently started a blog called LinkedIn for Marketing (LinkedInformarketing.com) because I was getting so many questions on how to use LinkedIn. I did one post on LinkedIn that said, "Here's how you use it." And, I'm getting up to 700 people per day just from LinkedIn people visiting this blog and subscribing to my RSS feed and e-mail. Now, they're saying, "Can you help me set it up? Can you come and train my company?"

If somebody goes to your blog and you don't have a place where they can subscribe to your RSS feed or your newsletter, you're going to lose about 95 percent of your traffic. Again, this is automated so that you don't have to write them every week or manage a list. Once they sign up for your list, you put them on an auto responder. It is very inexpensive to do this. These are e-mail responses that are set up by you in advance and as soon as someone signs up on your list they get an automatic message from you. You can set different e-mails to go out on different days with different information. If you have news you want to send out, you can blast it to them manually.

Even if you're busy or on vacation or at a conference or trade show, they will still get your e-mails. Auto responders are customizable to their name, as well.

*Before a business jumps in to social networking, are there any pitfalls that they might not be thinking of?*

**JO:** The learning curve can be huge, so it's a good thing they are reading this book. If you don't follow these steps, then you will be social networking a year from now wondering what happened to your time and business. Also, give yourself simple goals to start in regard to how much time you put into it daily. Allocate one day for an hour to set up your profiles, the next day to join groups, the following day to add connections, etc. The most important thing is that you get started.

# Case Study 4:

## Scott Stratten, Un-Marketing, Toronto, Canada

Scott was an early adapter of social media strategies starting with Ryze.com—an early online business networking site—about seven years ago. Today, Stratten has channeled the power of Twitter to help companies position themselves in front of their markets by using alternative marketing methods.

Here is Scott Stratten's social-networking story in his own words:

*Why do you focus on Twitter rather than sites like LinkedIn or Facebook?*

**SS:** One of the reasons why we focus 95 percent of our concentration on Twitter versus something like LinkedIn or even Facebook is that LinkedIn especially is a closed-door network, meaning you have to get an introduction to somebody before you can even get to know them or get involved with them really. You can't interact with them until you have been invited. You can also ask for an invitation but you might not get it. Twitter is more of an open door networking style, where you simply start following somebody because they are interesting, you can reply to their posts, start conversations and get to know them.

On Facebook, by way of contrast, I have to approve you as a Friend. And that term alone can especially throw people off in business because you are saying, "I have to approve you before I can get to know you," which to me is backwards.

I joined Twitter eight months ago and casually did it and got 2,000 followers in about eight months. I realized there was a great potential to get to know people at arm's length without having to get permission.

To start, I told myself I was going to focus on Twitter for 30 days. I made Twitter and building relationships my job for that month. In about six weeks I went from 2,000 followers to 10,000. You cannot build a network of remotely that size in that span of time on Facebook or LinkedIn or MySpace or anywhere else. I sent no newsletters out. I used no automated technique. People have followed me one at a time, it has been a total organic growth in six weeks and I have found there is nothing outside of Twitter that can do that, and I have been online since 1994.

*What are the pitfalls of going for the mass follow? Are there legitimate shortcuts to gaining that many followers?*

**SS:** The problem with the mass follow is there really are no shortcuts to social media success. If all you are going to do is try to grow a mass number of people then the only people to follow you in those systems are other people trying just to grow mass numbers. They are not communicating with each other. They are not building relationships. They are just trying to grow a number machine and that is like having a newsletter list where nobody reads what you are saying. It doesn't make any sense. To me there is no short-cut, automated wise, to success.

*What would you say to someone with limited or no experience on social network sites? They have no idea what Twitter is and are wondering how it help their business.*

**SS:** That was my attitude right from the beginning, "OK, great. What is the Twitter thing?" It is a bunch of people posting 140 characters, who cares? Then I realized that Twitter is the conversation that is going on now. For example, I joined in the conversation right as I was launching a six-week online workshop, it immediately was filled to capacity simply through letting people on Twitter know. This was a test run of my workshop, however, I filled it with paying customers, all solely through Twitter followers. I have also booked six large conferences in the next 6 months, strictly through my presence on Twitter.

*Are these paid speaking engagements you are talking about?*

**SS:** Yes, they are a combination of paid gigs or gigs that are in front of my market. I would not have gotten any of these bookings if I wasn't on Twitter.

*How many people do you follow? What are you getting from their content? What are you giving to your followers?*

**SS:** My goal on Twitter was to find other business owners out there that I could create relationships with and therefore learn from them, align with them, brainstorm with them, do joint ventures, and share markets and/or lists. I can increase my reach and vice versa, they can increase theirs with my followers. Now I know business owners from around the world. I wouldn't have been able to connect with them and share their reach through any other method. It is like a net-working event, except you are on your computer. So I follow people that I find interesting and therefore they follow me if they find me interesting.

*What specifically are you posting? How frequently are you posting and what type of content are you putting on there?*

**SS:** You want to do a combination of things on Twitter. I will, as they say, "tweet," which is put a message out there, a statement, something that I think will help people learn something about how to build relationships or something along those lines. If my followers like what I post they may do what is called a retweet, which takes you directly to their list of followers and it keeps moving. This can increase the number of people who want to read me, because they just learned from what I said, so they want to follow me now. It is important to combine good-content tweets along with a few personal posts and things that will make people laugh. Humor always works.

*How many people are you following currently?*

**SS:** I am following about 10,000 people. You can do one of two things to follow people, you can get a notification and check out the profile of people who follow you to see if you want to follow them, but I don't do that, because I get anywhere from 100 to 300 new followers a day and I just don't have time to go and look at everybody. The second option is called an auto-follow, if somebody follows me, I will follow them back, because I don't have time to look at their profiles. I can't keep up with 10,000 people talking, but what I can do is I use a program called Tweet Deck and that is at Tweetdeck.com. It is a free program; it puts it in columns for me. So every time somebody mentions me or replies to me, I see that in my deck and I can reply back to them. I can't keep up with all the people talking at once and trying to follow all these conversations, but I can follow the conversations that people are initiating with me. I also have what I referred to as a Rock Star column where you can specify who you want to follow more closely, so it is a specialized group of people I have a great relationship with now or I want one. I can put them in that one so I can follow them more closely.

*What about the business owners that says, "I already know how to do what I do, why would I want to follow more people that are doing the same thing?"*

**SS:** If a person feels that they have nothing else to learn in business and they just want to sell their product or a service or they just want more customers, they have no business being involved with social networking. If that is your mindset, it just won't work for you. On the other side of that, if you are looking to improve your skills and relationships, social media is going to help you in ways that you never imagined. Besides, most people on Twitter will not be your direct competition because they are not local to you, but together you can form a group of experts in your field.

*Let's look at pitfalls for the business owner that finally says, "Alright I buy it, I am going to jump in and get started." What should they be looking out for?*

**SS:** First you have got to clarify your intent when you go on there. What is it that you want to accomplish on Twitter? Is it to build an alliance, to build a brand, or to fill a funnel; what is it going to be? And if you realize your intent is to get to know people, then you have to commit to that plan of action by taking specific times of the day or a particular amount of time each week to look for other people with similar interests. If you want to get started on Twitter you will have to commit to it because the hardest thing to do in social media is to get started. The first 500 to 1,000 followers are the most difficult to get because you have no momentum. Join Twitter and place a Twitter search. Start at search.twitter.com and search a topic and you find people talking about it, then you just start following those people and jump into the conversation.

*What about localization? What are some ways on Twitter that you can keep the conversations local or take advantage outside of your local area?*

**SS:** You can go to twitter.grader.com and that will show you the highest active and ranked people in your local area or Twitterlocal.net. You can put it down to a town or a city or up to an entire country. Once you figure out who the local active members are, follow them and start a conversation with them. Talk about things based in your area if you are trying to attract local members. Once you build a relationship with them you can even take it further and go have coffee, these types of meetings will increase your presence and credibility in your community.

*Do you have anything in terms of basic step one, two, three to summarize the process?*

**SS:** Go to Twitter.com, create your profile, put a bio in there, along with your picture and your website. Next you need to extend a couple Tweets like, "hey new to Twitter, looking forward to learning this," along with a couple of ideas. Then search for some other people who are talking about either an interest of yours or that are in your local area.

It can be daunting when you are brand new and have no followers but just create your profile and then just start looking around and reading. When you find somebody who is active in your area, reply to them on Twitter and say, "Hey Jeff, I am new to Twitter, but I am also from San Luis Obispo, any tips for somebody who is new?" That starts the conversation and many times that person who is a Twitter veteran who has been on there for awhile, will sent out a tweet to everybody saying, "Hey, welcome Scott to Twitter, he is new so say hi, especially if you are from San Luis Obispo."

Lastly, you need to focus on building your following because when you follow people, they will get a notification that you have added them to follow and they will come check you out, they just might follow you back.

*What about people who are still skeptical about investing so much time into something so new. This could be a fad, it could be gone next year. How would you answer that?*

**SS:** The thing about that is there are no fads in building relationships. For instance ryze.com was a great tool, then the momentum kind of drained from it and they changed the site around a bit so we stopped using it, but I didn't stop having the relationships that I had already built. So use it for now, there are always going to be new tools. You know last year Facebook was a huge explosion, the year before that MySpace was the wonder child of the year before that it was LinkedIn and now it is Twitter. Things evolve, things change, but the relationships you make don't go away, so use it now, use it to your advantage.

# Case Study 5:

## TC McClenning, Public Relations Agency, Top Cat Creative Services, Topcatcreative.com

TC was a well-connected professional for years—getting the majority of her clients from her professional networks. In the last three months she has embraced LinkedIn and has more than 200 contacts and four groups. McClenning is also about to publish a book in a career series for real estate agents called *All in the Day's Work* that will cover some of the funny and crazy things that happened to her many real estate clients throughout the course of their work. She is planning to release the next book in the series for women in specialized professional areas such as nursing.

Here is TC McClenning's social-networking story in her own words:

**TC:** I feel like social networking is a relatively new area worth exploring. I decided to sign up on Facebook, Classmates, and LinkedIn some time ago, but I didn't utilize them. I was fortunate because I knew a lot of people in the industry who were working a lot and many of my clients came from their referrals. It was something I didn't really go out and actively pursue, and didn't feel that I needed to. I was just extremely busy at the time, and then, my field like just about every industry right now began to slow.

I decided to start focusing on LinkedIn in particular, because I felt it was more of a business-associated networking system than the others. I looked at all the groups that are available on the site, and signed up for groups of interest. I began building my connections list and in doing so, I was actually able to come into contact with people whom I had known in my local market sometime back and had lost contact. They had started a company or were still working with a company that was my client. I was able to reconnect with a couple of them and it resulted in some business. I am still in the early stage of online networking, I just started to do serious work on my LinkedIn profile and connections in December '08. In just one month, I already have over 200 contacts and my list is growing daily.

I think the only caution I would give is that one can really get sucked into social networking and spend some serious time. You have to balance yourself and your time when you get involved with social networking. One thing I have found extremely helpful is that there is a group on LinkedIn for just about anything you could possibly want to do, whether it is personal or professional interest. There are alumni groups for just about any college you may have graduated from. There are business groups that are either for women in a given state or area.

*For readers who might be thinking right now, why would someone spend four hours on a social-networking site, what advice would you offer them?*

**TC:** Set boundaries, allocate time, and stick to it. It is easy to say to yourself, "Oh well, I will just do this for a little while," and then two hours have passed and you are like "Oh, my gosh!"

*What are you generally doing that takes up that amount of time?*

**TC:** You can get involved with the various groups available. There are discussions wherein you may add your own question because you find it a helpful way to gain information for yourself on just about any topic. Whether you are trying to build a website and you have questions, or you want to know what is the best way to network or how you can attract a particular kind of client. You can ask any type of question. Some groups are more active than others, some may post 10 or 20 questions a day, and you can get caught up in responding to each of them while trying to expand your connections list. That can be very, very time consuming. Participating in groups is how I have been able to grow my list and that is what others are doing as well. It is a great way to get connected to people that you never would know or meet. There are so many possibilities. It has been just two months and I feel like I am just barely cracking the surface. For example, I met you. And I have connected with a couple of people with whom I had lost touch, and they became clients.

These social-networking sites are not hard to do. They can be quite interesting actually and you can learn something from each of them daily. I have found LinkedIn to be quite helpful, I think everybody has a little more time than we would like to right now, and an hour a day on the site may be a profitable investment of your time. As I said before, the set-up period, just getting yourself submersed in what feature to get in and just starting your connections is a little time-intensive for the first month or so, but I know that investment has been very helpful to me.

# Case Study 6:

## Stuart Crawford, Vice President of Business Development for Bulletproof InfoTech, Red Deer and Calgary, Alberta, Canada, www.bulletproofit.ca

Bulletproof does small business computer network support for companies that are between five to 100 employees. The company basically becomes the "computer guy" for small businesses. The IT consultants at Bulletproof pick up the responsibility of maintaining everything computer-related so the business owner can focus on all the other things in their business that they have to worry about. Included in their key services is helping these small businesses understand the world of social media and social networking through "lunch and learn" sessions and training seminars. In addition to face-to-face trainings, Bulletproof uses the media that they teach about in as part of these trainings—offering some of the sessions via podcasts, webcasts, and blogs.

Here is Stuart Crawford's social-networking story in his own words:

*When did you decide that you needed to incorporate social networking into your business model?*

**SC:** I realized that if I am going on Google and I am going on other search engines to find information, I am sure the customers that I want to reach are doing the exact same thing.

It is great to have a good website but people have to visit that site if they are going to buy your goods and services.

The question became, "What other ways can we drive people to our site?" The answer is to get out there and to become the recognized expert in our field. To that end, I run a series of blogs. I have my own personal blog that is kind of like a Jerry Seinfeld episode, some days I talk about nothing and some days I cover some great content. The important thing is to get people connecting with you on a personal level and then becoming an industry expert on the value of technology in small business. The days of directly selling a product—"I have this product, and you have to buy it"—are long over and we use social media as a way to drive the proposition of why something will help a business instead of pushing a product. Again, using social-networking applications, if we are doing something cool, we can share with seven other people and they can put it on their blogs, podcasts, and Twitter. It is another great way to build momentum for our business.

*What social networks specifically have you engaged in?*

**SC:** I am quite heavily on Twitter. I started developing my contact list about two months ago and I have about 400 contacts already. I also have 1,200 friends on Facebook. I have set up an automated system, my blog feeds Twitter and then Twitter feeds Facebook automatically.

*How do you do that?*

**SC:** The website is called tweeterfeed.com. You can put in your RSS feed from your blog and it will replicate it to your Twitter. Then there is an application in Facebook to put your Twitter updates into Facebook. As soon as I started doing that, the readership on my blog increased 10 times. Put a snappy title on your blog entry and people will click the link on Twitter to read the entire blog entry. It is important to note once you have a blog, it was when you added the components of the social networks to that blog that the traction really started to take off.

*How would you suggest a business get started with social networking?*

**SC:** It really depends on who their target audience is. If you are interested in business-to-business-type transactions, LinkedIn would be a good place to get out there, get a profile, and start participating in some of the groups. Start by answering questions for people rather than pushing your products—it is no different than networking face-to-face.

Answering questions and participating will allow people to get to know you and they will ask what services you provide and you can grow your business that way. If your focus is business to consumer, set up a blog, set up a Facebook account, get on Twitter, and start coordinating them all, feeding your blog to Twitter and to Facebook.

*Is there any other advice that you could offer our readers? Pitfalls? Things to avoid?*

**SC:** The biggest thing with social networking is to make sure you do not become a salesperson online. Education is always a good way to help people, make an investment in their challenge, and keep yourself real. Don't hide behind an alias, people want to do business with the individual not the corporation.

Keep it real and keep it professional—maybe leave out the pictures of you being drunk in the bar with friends. Be aware that people check social-networking sites to get a feel for who you are. When I am looking to hire people now, I look them up on Facebook and all the social-networking sites. We use social networking in two ways, a way to get information out about us and also a way to get research done on people we are looking at doing business with or hire to join our team.

# Case Study 7:
## Paula Pollock, Pollock Marketing Group, paulapollock.com and paulapollock.wordpress.com

Paula is a marketing consultant originally working with small to medium businesses in her local area. When the economy really starting to crumble in 2007 she decided to go national and realized the best way to do that would be to use social networking. After only six months, she has more business than she knows what to do with!

Here's Paula Pollock's social-networking story in her own words:

*At what point did you decide to incorporate social networking into your business-building model?*

**PP:** When the economy was starting to take a turn, I decided to take my services national, basically go big or stay home. I stepped up my blog, posted it in more places. Social media is by no means something to do if you have no time on your hands. It is time-consuming; there's no doubt about that. I started my social-networking efforts and now I have my virtual assistant doing it for me. 50 percent of your time will go to writing valuable content with a catchy subject heading because no one's going to open or read something that doesn't sound enticing and the remaining 50 percent goes to posting and replies.

*What sites do you engage in?*

**PP:** I put my main efforts in to LinkedIn. My second choice is Facebook and then I write articles and post on additional sites such as Articles.com and Helium where content buyers look for information.

*Are you posting one blog post and then distributing that to the different venues or are you posting different content to different sites?*

**PP:** It depends on the content topic as to what group or site I am going to post on. I try to keep it the same and post throughout the different sites; however, sometimes I write industry-specific articles that don't belong on certain sites or in certain posting areas on a social-networking site.

*Are you posting manually, or do you have an automated system when you post to your blog, it goes to various sites?*

**PP:** Anyone who subscribes to our RSS feed automatically gets it and my blog is fed out to Twitter as well as Facebook. Currently discussion groups don't have an option for that so I have to manually post. It will only take me about 15–20 minutes to copy and paste the same post into the different groups.

*Tell us more about the virtual assistant who does this for you now? How does that work?*

**PP:** I have built my social networking to a point where it is profitable and there are not enough hours in my day to work with clients and still do this marketing. I still do the writing; however, my VA posts and monitors.

*How often are you updating your content?*

**PP:** At least once a week, sometimes twice a week depending on what the demands are online in regard to request for content and resources.

*Other than posting, what types of other activities are you doing on the social-networking sites?*

**PP:** I comment in discussion groups on LinkedIn, as well. In order to build your credibility online you have to interact. With Twitter, it can be a little faster because it is live conversation, and your post is limited to 140 characters. However, with that said, I have seen someone post a call for speakers on Twitter and I responded to that post immediately.

*How long have you been social networking?*

**PP:** Social networking has been a huge part of my business for at least the past six months and it has grown my business to levels that I didn't even imagine were possible through this type of medium.

*What type of specific results have you received from your social-networking efforts?*

**PP:** Our opt-in subscribers have probably tripled which has also resulted in paid business.

*Are you incorporating what you've learned in the last six months into what you're recommending to your clients?*

**PP:** Absolutely; without a doubt. The hardest hurdle for them to overcome is probably the time element and, getting them to overcome the perceived barrier that they can't write. You're talking about topics that you know, so it should come fairly easy.

*For people who say, "I am just a mom and pop local business, I don't need to be doing this," what's your response to that?*

**PP:** If you don't join the conversation online, someone else in your local market will, so be first to do it. You don't have to be the best, but be the first.

*What would you say to people who respond with "I'm behind the curve, I don't know this technology and I'm not going to be able to catch up"?*

**PP:** Just find your niche online. There's a reason why you're still in business vs. your competitor. For example, if you are a local coffee cafe competing with Starbucks on every corner, how will you differentiate yourself? Well, how do you differentiate yourself now against Starbucks in the marketplace? Do you charge the same high prices? Do you focus on more of a local niche? Do you offer free Wi-Fi? Talk about these things online, let people know about it. Don't try to be Starbucks. Talk about what is going on in the community. Do you think that Starbucks is doing that?

*Compare social networking to traditional marketing techniques.*

*PP:* Social networking is a time investment, traditional ways can cost you time and money. Look at what you have been doing. How well is it working? What are the results? You will probably find that traditional techniques are no longer bringing in the amount of business that they used to. No matter how you are marketing your business, you should have some type of tracking system in place to monitor the results.

The one exception I have found is businesses that are focused on baby boomers should still keep a balance of the traditional Yellow Page–type of advertising because the 55 and over crowd still loves the Yellow Pages.

In closing, you just need to get started, try it out, get your feet wet. It might seem a bit scary at first, but it's really not bad once you dive in.

# Case Study 8:

## Tony DeRico, Profit Hunters International, www.profithunters.biz

DeRico's business has two sides: a sports side and a business coaching and consulting side. Profit Hunters' partner company, Winslow Research Institute, developed a human behavior assessment system that has helped a diverse range of clients from professional athletes to top high tech companies like Oracle. The common denominator is the desire to enhance performance. As a business to business company, Profit Hunters experimented with LinkedIn and other sites for business until almost 20 percent of its current business is being generated from social-networking connections.

Here is Tony DeRico's social-networking story in his own words:

*At what point did you decide to enter the social-networking area as part of your communications and marketing program?*

**TD:** It started with an invite to LinkedIn. I accepted, but never did much with it. About four months later there was one connection that was more marketing-directed, and I decided to explore using this vehicle to reach out and connect with like-minded people and/or clients. I went on to Plaxo and The Academy, which is a predominantly European social network, and then we started to explore more of these industry-specific social networks. Honestly, I have only been active for about four months.

*What have you accomplished in that relatively short time?*

**TD:** We are now in negotiations with several companies in India. We are also working with a couple of consulting companies that have asked us to come to India and they're going to arrange for presentations to consulting companies that might have a need for this sort of service, and for a broad range of their clients to assist them. In North America, in just a matter of months, we have brought on at least a dozen clients, and probably half a dozen distributors that wanted to use our services.

*What percentage of new business would you say you've garnered through social networking?*

**TD:** At this point, at least 20 percent of the total business. However, I'm finding that it's a very effective way to communicate and connect with like-minded people, and then simply set up a time to communicate, explore common interests, and then decide whether or not to move forward in a business relationship.

*What were you doing previously to make these same kinds of connections?*

**TD:** We did some advertising and a number of shows. In addition to trade shows, we attended a few local Chamber of Commerce events. We can now reach out to larger groups online than we can in person. We still have a balance of the two.

*Have you cut back on any of those other traditional efforts since you began social networking?*

**TD:** We've have eliminated print collateral pieces as well as cutting back on print advertising as we have gotten little to no response from them.

*Can you give us a step-by-step as to how we might achieve the same success?*

**TD:** On LinkedIn, you need to join groups that have some commonality. I suggest that you join in some of the conversations as well. I still believe that there is phenomenal value for connecting on voice-to-voice level, versus strictly chatting online, so I often ask to set up a quick chat with people I feel we can do business with. Continue to expand your network connections and stay active on the sites that you are on.

*Do you recommend that businesses put together a social-networking plan before jumping online?*

**TD:** I think it depends on the business focus. No matter what, social networking is addictive, if you don't create a plan at some point you are going to look up from your computer and one month may have just passed you by. I also suggest that businesses are selective on the sites they go on so that they do not waste valuable time.

*Does it really matter how many friends, followers, or connections that you have? Is it all about numbers?*

**TD:** I think it is more important to build trust-based relationships. I would rather have quality relationships with 50 people that I am doing business with rather than having 2,500 people on my network that I am not actively doing business with.

# Case Study 9:
## Charles Wankel, Associate Professor, St. John's University, Queens, NY

Charles describes himself as "perhaps the most networked management professor in the world. I live, breathe, and thrive on social networking." He is currently working on *Management Through Collaboration: Teaming in the Networked World* (Rutledge Publications) due out in January 2010 (www.globally-colaborating.com). The project involves 930 co-authors from 90 countries—including Tonga, Iran, Botswana, Peru, Grenada, and India—creating a large virtual team. Wankel found these people through LinkedIn and Facebook and emphasized in his interview that it would have been impossible to move forward in such a robust way without locating his collaborators through social networking.

Here's Charles Wankel's social-networking story in his own words:

**CW:** I think the idea for most people is that they are getting along pretty well without joining LinkedIn or Facebook, so why should they bother? Furthermore, social-networking sites do not come with a rule book or set of instructions. Rather it's something you have to either be taught or learn through a book like this one, leading the way for people.

In my case of using LinkedIn, the book project, one of the things I wanted to do was to have several thousand video interviews with managers around the world. Some of the case studies are about incidents that happened in different companies—about how they were solved and so on. In building my team and connections, I realized that I needed somebody that can help me create thousands of YouTube videos. This somebody needed to be willing to do this and wait for the royalties to get paid. I went to LinkedIn and using terms like YouTube and online video and new media I went through several hundred people through my searches. I found about 20 that I thought would be good and I started to contact them. I worked my way through a few, then I came across J. Sibley Law, he headed up a motion picture and film company called Saxon Mills, LLC. This company had been honored by the Webby awards in 2007 for one of their YouTube programs. He was somebody at world-class level and that had worked with major *Fortune* 100 companies. Fortunately, he seemed intrigued by the idea and saw these videos as maybe constituting a program for YouTube for him. He said he would be coming into the New York area in the near future and we agreed to meet. How would I have met this person any other way?

*How many connections do you have on the different networks?*

**CW:** I have more than 3,000 connections on LinkedIn and 600 on Facebook. I established my connections on Linkedin by typing in words like "president" into the title field so that I could get presidents and vice presidents of companies. Another key word that I used was "professor" or "higher education." For my Facebook, I used search features, as well.

*What advice would you give to entrepreneurs who are new to social networking?*

**CW:** You need to be careful when you are building your networks to not connect with people that misrepresent themselves. You might find someone who claims to be someone they are not. People will not know if you've disconnected from them or if you do not accept their invite so don't worry about offending people. Just be safe and cautious, that's all. You may not come across this often but you need to at least be aware that these types of people are out there.

# Case Study 10:

## Starr Hall, International Publicist, Starr Hall Inc., San Luis Obispo, CA, www.starrhall.com

(Due to my ongoing social-networking success and the reason I wrote this book, I decided to add my own case study, participant disclosure does not apply for this case study.)

Starr started her PR and branding agency in 2005 with just two clients after walking away from an executive position at a well-known advertising agency. Within 18 months, Starr built her agency to over 70 active clients worldwide. Her recent successes through social-networking over the past two years have led her to international speaking engagements, book deals, corporate on-site trainings and the sale of her agency, 2 Point Media, to a national agency, Whizbang. One hundred percent of her business continued to come directly from social networking.

Here's Starr Hall's social-networking story in her own words:

**SH:** In 2006, I came to realize that the media and marketing landscape were changing and fast. In order to keep up with technology changing daily and keeping my clients in front of their markets I had no choice but to jump online and learn at the time what I referred to as the beast—social networking.

Within the first few weeks of jumping online I knew that I had to start focusing most of my efforts into social networking. I was watching the conversations happening, getting involved, and then boom, business started to come my way. The more active I was online, the more connections that I made and the more business came through the door.

*What type of business did you get from your initial social-networking efforts?*

**SH:** I was getting anything from booking paid speaking engagements to new consulting clients. I also have products such as eBooks, online webinars, podcasts, and trainings, and people would land on my site and buy. In addition, I started to form partnerships around the world whether it was with another consulting firm in another country or a company that wanted me to provide ongoing social-networking trainings to their clients.

*What activities do you do online that cause this type of business to come in?*

**SH:** First of all, I have a blog on my website. It is very important to have an active blog so that you can interact with the online world and provide valuable content that is of interest to your target market. For example, one of the posts that I did was "The Top Five Mistakes People Make with Social Networking." I posted this title onto the major sites—LinkedIn, Twitter, and Facebook—with a link back to my blog that contained the actual top five mistakes. In addition, I offered a free report on the subject that had an e-mail capture. This is how I collected and built my e-mail list. Within about seven days, I had close to 1,200 e-mails from this post, conversations happening online about me and my posting and people that were not even my connections were posting my site all over their networks. This was from *one* post.

*What sites are you active on for your business?*

**SH:** Because I am a consultant and speaker it is important for me to stay active on LinkedIn, Twitter, and Facebook. This is where my main focus is. I do, however, monitor new sites that are popping up to see if I should be on them. A new site that just popped up recently is blitztime.com, I went ahead and put a profile up and I visited weekly to see if I need to build my focus and network on this site. I did jump on to Plaxo and XING. I haven't really worked those networks so I will probably jump off of those soon if I don't see much activity.

*What are your connection numbers on each site currently, and how long did it take you to build to those numbers?*

**SH:** My LinkedIn connections are currently in the 700s, Facebook is in the 400s, and my Twitter followers are close to 1,500. To me it is not really about the quantity, it is about the quality of relationships that you build. If I can connect with a few leaders on Twitter that have 50,000 followers and they like the content I am posting, they will retweet (aka forward it) to their network. I don't even have to work to build those kind of numbers, I just need to connect with connectors and bring them into my network and share connections as they do for me.

*What advice would you give to someone who has been social networking for a year and hasn't seen any results?*

**SH:** Without even talking to them I know that they are not providing enough value content in their area of expertise and they are not building relationships. If you are not getting business off of social-networking sites then you must just be on there for a popularity contest or to read other peoples content and posts. You need to build relationships and trust before anyone is going to hire you or buy your products, period.

# Social Networking Glossary

**Aggregation** The process of gathering content from blogs and other websites with RSS feeds. The results of aggregation may be displayed in an aggregator website like MyYahoo! or Google Reader, or directly on your desktop.

**Avatar** An online persona; a graphical representation of the user.

**Back channel** Private communications (e-mails or other messages) sent by the facilitator or between individuals during public conferencing.

**Blog, short for "web log"** Blogs are technically a website used as an online journal. When you add an entry to a blog you are "blogging" and the person who owns the blog is a "blogger."

**Blogosphere** A term to describe the universe of blogs on the Internet, and the conversations taking place within that sphere.

**Blogroll** A list of sites displayed in the sidebar of a blog, showing what the blogger reads on a regular basis.

**Champions** Participants in an online community who get conversations and discussions started by posting messages, responding, and helping others.

**Chat** The act of communicating in text online. It can be one-on-one or to a group. To chat online you need an application or software like Google Chat, Yahoo! Messenger, MSN, AIM, or Skype. Unlike e-mail, chat allows you to have real time conversations in text. Real time video chat is becoming ubiquitous. (See *Instant Messaging*.)

**Comments** Comments on blogs. Comment boxes are usually located beneath blog posts.

**Communities** Groups of people who primarily communicate through the Internet. Online communities may use formalized e-mail lists or forums to communicate, or they may evolve around or among bloggers, or on social networking sites.

**E-mail lists** E-mail lists, or groups, are important tools in social networking. They give the ability to blast a message from a central postbox to any number of subscribers, and for them to respond, driving traffic to a desired location.

**Face-to-face (f2f)** Term that describes people meeting offline.

**Facilitators** Members of social networks who moderate conversations to keep them on topic and prod further discussion about a topic.

**Feeds** Allow users to read, view, or listen to items from blogs and other RSS-enabled sites without having to visit the site. Generally provided by subscribing to an aggregator that contains the content of an item.

**Forums** Discussion areas on websiteswhere people can post messages or comment on existing messages.

**Friends** In social networking sites, friends are contacts whose profiles are linked to your profile. In some networks users have to accept the link before it is added to their profile, some do not require confirmation.

**HTML (HyperText Markup Language)** Provides a means to describe the attributes and structure of text-based information in a document. Can include embedded scripting language code (such as JavaScript). It's relatively simple, written in the form of tags within angle brackets (e.g., < b > for bold).

**Instant messaging (IM)** A private chat with another individual through programs like AOL Instant Messenger, or Google Chat. A rapid exchange method that's a good alternative to e-mail, as users can also select whether they appear online or available to talk. (See *Chat.*)

**Internet** A global collection of computers joined together in networks. These interconnected computer networks allow for the rapid exchange of information via telephone wires and satellites. The Internet has services such as the World Wide Web and e-mail.

**Lurkers** Members of social networks who read forums or blogs but rarely contribute or add comments to forums.

**Membership** Belonging to a group.

**Newsreaders** Websites or desktop tools that act as aggregators, gathering content from blogs and similar sites using RSS feeds, enabling the user to read items from multiple sites without having to visit each one individually.

**Open-source software** Any computer software whose source code lets users change and improve the software, and to redistribute it in modified or unmodified form.

**P2P (peer-to-peer) communication** Refers to two computers in a network set up to transmit and share data. The computers are "peers," or equals, and file sharing is allowed, so usually security between these "nodes" isn't very tight.

**Permalink** The permanent link to an item of content, like a blog post, rather than to a website with updating and changing content.

**Photo and/or video sharing** Occurs on websites that allow users to store, print, and share files with others.

**Podcast** Audio or video content that's periodically updated and automatically downloaded through a subscription so that users can view or listen to the cast offline.

**Post** An item on a blog or forum.

**Professional network** A kind of online social network devoted to job seekers and potential employers who want to find each other based on common interests; LinkedIn, for example.

**Profile** An online form that provides other network members with personal information about you, such as educational background, interests, hobbies. Depending on the network, users can specify profiles as "private," or viewed by members only.

**Question-and-Answer Networks** A type of niche social network that lets users connect and exchange information. Members pose a question, and other members provide the answer for free. Some are forums or discussion groups, while others allow instant online chat.

**RSS (Really Simple Syndication)** A function on a website that lets users subscribe to content and receive RSS feeds from a website. Commonly used with blogs.

**Sharing** Offering other people the use of your text, images, bookmarks, or other uploaded content.

**Social bookmarking** Users on a social network who want to share their Internet bookmarks use a service called social bookmarking. Users save the URLs of web pages, videos, and photos, and keep them in lists called bookmarks. They then make this information accessible to other network members arranged by category, tags, or topic.

**Social media** Refers to the tools and platforms that people use to share content online (e.g., blogs, podcasts, photo sharing sites, wikis, etc.)

**Social networking** Groups of websites that let users interact as members of an online community. Social networking revolutionized the way people communicate with each other over the Internet.

**Social networks** Online places where people with similar interests can interact via e-mail, chat, and instant messaging. Depending on what features the particular social network offers, users can also blog, share files, and form discussion groups or forums.

**Social news** As part of the online social networking phenomenon, these websites let users add news items. In that sense, they "make" the news or choose which items are worthy for mention.

# Social Networking Glossary

**Tag** A word that describes a piece of information, such as a web page or blog entry. Tags allow the item to be found by others using a search engine like Google. Tags can also be used to describe a bookmark or the location of a website.

**Threads** Strands of conversation on a topic. On a web forum they are most clearly defined as any item that's posted in a certain topic heading. On blogs they are less clearly defined, but emerge through webs of comments and trackbacks.

**Topic** In an online discussion, an idea, issue, or talking point in a conversation composed of threads. Forums are often sorted by topics.

**Viral advertising** Use of text messages, videos, or online games to advertise to social networks. The goal is that the advertising will be so popular that it spreads like a "virus" though word-of-mouth, e-mail, or text messaging.

**Web 2.0** Refers to the ongoing changes on the Internet, allowing for more user-generated content. Blogging, social networking, and search engine optimization are part of that evolution.

**Web site** A collection of text information, photos, or videos that reside on a web page on the Internet. As such, it has a location on the World Wide Web and can be found by others performing a search.

**Wiki** A set of web pages where anyone can modify or contribute content. Coined by Wikipedia, a massive, user-driven online encyclopedia.